NARRATIVE OF THE LIFE OF FREDERICK DOUGLASS

FREDERICK DOUGLASS was born Frederick Augustus Washington Bailey to Harriet Bailey, a slave woman, and an unknown white man, probably in February 1818. He spent his formative years between Baltimore and St Michaels, Maryland, working first as a servant in the home of Sophia and Hugh Auld and later as a brutalized farm worker. On 3 September 1838, barely 20 years old, Douglass escaped from Baltimore disguised in sailor's clothes. Soon after he married Anna Murray, a free black, and they settled in New Bedford, Massachusetts, where Douglass began work as an anti-slavery crusader. Following a speech at an anti-slavery convention in Nantucket in 1841, Douglass was hired by the Massachusetts Anti-Slavery Society to lecture about his life as a slave. So eloquent were his speeches that doubts raged as to whether he had actually been a slave. In an effort to stifle such rumours, Douglass wrote *Narrative of the Life of Frederick Douglass, an American Slave*, which became an instant and international bestseller. Fearing recapture and possible re-enslavement, Douglass fled to England, where he became a free man when a group of supporters purchased his freedom for $700. Douglass returned to the United States in the spring of 1847 and launched *The North Star*, his own newspaper (it was later renamed *Frederick Douglass' Paper*, and finally *Douglass' Monthly*). He published his second autobiography, *My Bondage and My Freedom* in 1855. Following the outbreak of the Civil War, Douglass successfully lobbied President Lincoln to permit black soldiers to enlist for the Union cause, and once the war was won, he fought for swift passage of the Fifteenth Amendment, guaranteeing suffrage to newly freed slaves. He served as federal marshall of the District of Columbia, president of the Freedman's Bureau Bank, consul to Haiti, and chargé d'affaires for the Dominican Republic. These and other experiences of his later life constituted the focus of this third autobiography, *Life and Times of Frederick Douglass* (1881). He died on 20 February 1895, shortly after delivering a speech at a women's rights rally.

DEBORAH E. MCDOWELL is Professor of English at the University of Virginia. The author of *'The Changing Same': Studies in Fiction by Black-American Women* and *Leaving Pipe Shop: Memories of Kin*, she is co-editor, with Arnold Rampersad, of *Slavery and the Literary Imagination*; period editor of the *Norton Anthology of African-American Literature*; and the author of numerous essays and reviews on African-American literature and culture.

OXFORD WORLD'S CLASSICS

*For over 100 years Oxford World's Classics have brought
readers closer to the world's great literature. Now with over 700
titles—from the 4,000-year-old myths of Mesopotamia to the
twentieth century's greatest novels—the series makes available
lesser-known as well as celebrated writing.*

*The pocket-sized hardbacks of the early years contained
introductions by Virginia Woolf, T. S. Eliot, Graham Greene,
and other literary figures which enriched the experience of reading.
Today the series is recognized for its fine scholarship and
reliability in texts that span world literature, drama and poetry,
religion, philosophy and politics. Each edition includes perceptive
commentary and essential background information to meet the
changing needs of readers.*

OXFORD WORLD'S CLASSICS

FREDERICK DOUGLASS

Narrative of the Life of Frederick Douglass
An American Slave

Edited with an Introduction by
DEBORAH E. McDOWELL

With Notes by
JOHN CHARLES

OXFORD
UNIVERSITY PRESS

OXFORD

UNIVERSITY PRESS

Great Clarendon Street, Oxford OX2 6DP

Oxford University Press is a department of the University of Oxford.
It furthers the University's objective of excellence in research, scholarship,
and education by publishing worldwide in

Oxford New York

Athens Auckland Bangkok Bogotá Buenos Aires Calcutta
Cape Town Chennai Dar es Salaam Delhi Florence Hong Kong Istanbul
Karachi Kuala Lumpur Madrid Melbourne Mexico City Mumbai
Nairobi Paris São Paulo Singapore Taipei Tokyo Toronto Warsaw

with associated companies in Berlin Ibadan

Oxford is a registered trade mark of Oxford University Press
in the UK and in certain other countries

Published in the United States
by Oxford University Press Inc., New York

Introduction, Note on the Text, Select Bibliography
© Deborah E. McDowell 1999
Chronology © William L. Andrews 1999
Explanatory Notes © John Charles 1999

British Library Cataloguing in Publication Data

Data available

Library of Congress Cataloging in Publication Data

Data available

ISBN 978–0–19–953907–9

18

Typeset by RefineCatch Ltd, Bungay, Suffolk
Printed in Great Britain by
Clays Ltd, Elcograf S.p.A.

CONTENTS

CONTENTS

INTRODUCTION

When the Boston Anti-Slavery Society published *Narrative of the Life of Frederick Douglass, An American Slave*, in May 1845, the 27-year-old ex-slave had already distinguished himself as a lecturer on the abolitionist circuit. Douglass inaugurated what would become an illustrious oratorical career in August 1841, when he rose to speak at an anti-slavery convention in Nantucket, Massachusetts. At that point, he was but a scant three years removed from slavery, having escaped to Massachusetts from Baltimore, Maryland in 1838, disguised in sailor's clothes. Stenographic transcripts of his addresses, published in various newspapers, reported enthusiastic responses—'cheers', 'hear, hears', 'loud applause', and 'sensation'—from capacity crowds, who listened, according to one reporter, 'with marked attention', to speeches that sometimes averaged two hours long.

Douglass's spectacular success as the anti-slavery movement's most eloquent and electrifying speaker repeatedly aroused the suspicion of sceptics who alleged that he was an impostor, doubting that one so recently escaped from slavery could be so charismatic, could summon such stinging and commanding denunciations of slavery. In order to quell these suspicions, or, as Douglass put it in one of his speeches, 'to set [himself] right before the public in the United States', he wrote the *Narrative*, presenting the 'whole facts of [his] case'.[1]

Douglass named names and places, detailed slavery's horrible cruelties and yet suspicions persisted. Sceptics were not persuaded by Douglass's bold subtitle, 'written by himself', or by the testimony of Wendell Phillips and William Lloyd Garrison, both prominent and respected members of the Boston Anti-Slavery

---

[1] Quotations from 'Emancipation Is an Individual, National, and an International Responsibility: An Address Delivered in London, England, on May 18, 1846' in John Blassingame (ed.), *The Frederick Douglass Papers*, i (New Haven: Yale University Press, 1979), 251.

Society.[2] While both men testified to the narrative's credibility, Garrison vouching in his preface that 'nothing has been set down in malice, nothing exaggerated, nothing drawn from the imagination', some readers still dismissed the *Narrative* as a forgery. In a letter to *The Liberator*, an anti-slavery magazine, one A. C. C. Thompson, a former slaveholder and neighbour of Thomas Auld, one of Douglass's owners, declared the book a 'budget of falsehoods from beginning to end'.[3] Thompson registered his doubts about the narrative in a letter to *The Liberator*, an anti-slavery magazine. Although meant to impugn Douglass's credibility, Thompson's letter, by claiming intimate knowledge of Douglass and the personalities of his *Narrative*, had unwittingly verified that Douglass had been, in fact, the slave he professed to be and not 'a free Negro' impersonating a slave. Other readers, some white Marylanders, lined up to attest to the *Narrative's* credibility, but, not taking their testimony for granted, Douglass referred remaining doubters to Timothy Dwight Weld's *American Slavery as It is: Testimony of a Thousand Witnesses* and to Charles Dickens's chapter on slavery in *American Notes*. These two sources would establish that his own acounts of slavery were not overblown.

During the era of the fugitive slave narrative Douglass's was not the only such narrative burdened with suspicions about its veracity. The *Memoirs of Archy Moore* (1836) brought great embarrassment to the abolitionists when the historian and abolitionist, Richard Hildreth, admitted that it was a fiction that he had concocted. Just two years later, in 1838, abolitionists were

---

[2] Ante-bellum slave narratives were frequently dictated to and written by white editors, some of whom had no connections to the abolitionist cause and no sympathy for the slave narrator. Douglass claimed sole authorship of his narratives, and when compared with his letters, speeches, and editorials, there is little doubt that he authored his own autobiographies. For a discussion of white editors and black slave narratives, see John Blassingame, 'Using the Testimony of Ex-Slaves: Approaches and Problems', in Charles T. Davis and Henry Louis Gates, Jr. (eds.), *The Slave's Narrative* (New York: Oxford University Press, 1985), 78–98 and William L. Andrews, *To Tell a Free Story: The First Century of Afro-American Autobiography; 1760–1865* (Champaign: University of Illinois Press, 1986), 19–22.

[3] See William L. Andrews and William S. McFeeley (eds.), *Narrative of the Life of Frederick Douglass, An American Slave, Written by Himself* (New York: W. W. Norton, 1977), 89.

dealt another embarrassing blow when the Massachusetts Anti-Slavery Society published the *Narrative of James Williams*, edited by the American poet John Greenleaf Whittier. When it too was eventually ruled a fabrication, the Executive Committee of the Massachusetts Anti-Slavery Society was forced to publish a retraction and withdraw the book from sale.

While the 1845 *Narrative* was never dishonoured as a forgery, latter-day historians have determined that Douglass took great liberties with the facts of his life—distorting, suppressing, occasionally inventing details and incidents in order, some have argued, to make the strongest possible case against the dehumanizing institution of slavery. In *Young Frederick Douglass: The Maryland Years*, for instance, Dickson J. Preston challenges Douglass's account of his early years as a slave in Talbot County, Maryland, while corroborating the many names and places he referred to in the *Narrative*. According to Preston, Douglass deals cryptically with his origins in the *Narrative*'s opening pages, devoting a mere few lines to his maternal genealogy and the 'strong and closely knit kin group with family pride and traditions' handed down to him by his grandmother, Betsey Bailey. 'Although they were illiterate, Eastern Shore slaves,' Preston continues, the 'Bailey clan into which [Douglass] was born were far from being "dregs of society".'

Douglass creates haunting and affecting impressions of suffering protracted hunger and cold, of being fed mush from a 'large wooden tray or trough' from which he and other children fed 'like so many pigs . . . some with oyster-shells, others with pieces of shingle, some with naked hands, and none with spoons' (p. 34). Preston also disputes this account, asserting that the picture Douglass painted of boyhood deprivation and cruelty was largely exaggerated. 'Far from being a deprived child,' Preston maintains, Douglass was 'exceptionally privileged', recognized early on as an 'unusually gifted boy . . . [who] was given opportunities open to few, if any, other young blacks.'[4]

---

[4] Dickson Preston, *Young Frederick Douglass: The Maryland Years* (Baltimore: Johns Hopkins University Press, 1980), pp. xiv, xv.

Although Preston's challenges to Douglass's 'facts' are significant corrections to the historical record, his emphasis on
Douglass's 'privileges' overlooks a more fundamental fact:
whatever 'special treatment' he may have received, Douglass was
still a slave. And within that context, 'privilege' becomes a bla-
tantly ironic and incongruous choice of words. That fact was
clearly not lost on Douglass, who pinpointed his situation in an
address delivered in Bridgwater, England in August 1846. Slavery
robbed him of the right to his own person, the right even to say,
'myself'. As the transcript of the speech reads, 'his head, his eyes,
his hands, his whole body . . . [and] his immortal spirit, were the
property of another'.[5] This was the 'fact' or 'truth' Douglass
propounded from public lectern to printed page. While the bulk
of his writings consist of speeches and editorials, to modern
readers Douglass's contribution to American history and letters
is contained, most compellingly, in the texts of his own life.
According to many, the 1845 *Narrative* is the jewel in the crown.[6]

I

By the time Douglass's *Narrative* appeared in 1845, first-person
narratives by African-Americans were an established genre.
Encompassing a range of sub-genres—spiritual autobiographies,
criminal confessions, captivity narratives, travel accounts, and
memoirs—they dated back to 1760, when *A Narrative of the
Uncommon Sufferings, and Surprizing Deliverance of Briton Ham-
mon, A Negro Man* was published. But not before the 1840s, the
era of the fugitive slave autobiographies, had African-American
'I' narratives garnered such popularity and commanded such

---

[5] Frederick Douglass, 'American Slavery and Britain's Rebuke of Manstealers: An
Address Delivered in Bridgwater, England, on 31 August 1846', in Blassingame (ed.),
The Frederick Douglass Papers, i. 365.

[6] Others, like Eric Sundquist, differ from this popular opinion, maintaining that 'an
estimate of [Douglass's] importance must rely not only on a single activity or narrative
but on the whole range of his life and work'. And while the *Narrative* is the most widely
read of Douglass's writings, Sundquist continues, 'there are definite limitations to it as a
revelation of Douglass's identity and thought.' See the introduction to Eric Sundquist
(ed.), *Frederick Douglass: New Literary and Historical Essays* (New York: Cambridge
University Press, 1990), 3, 4.

notice as a separate and esteemed category of American letters.[7]
Ephraim Peabody, a Boston Unitarian minister, was among the
first to herald what he termed this 'new department'—the autobiographies of ex-slaves—to the 'literature of civilization'.
Reviewing narratives by Douglass and Josiah Henson, Peabody
judged them both to be 'among the most remarkable productions
of the age'.[8]

Fugitive slave narratives added to a growing stock of first-
person accounts of shipwrecks, captivity by Indians, and various
sensational adventures, which ante-bellum Americans produced
and avidly consumed. Although Douglass's 1845 *Narrative*
appropriates various aspects of these and other genres popular in
ante-bellum America, it was *sui generis*. That it was the most
influential, the most widely reviewed and critically acclaimed of
the ante-bellum narratives partly attests to its uniqueness. The
book was an instant success, selling 5,000 copies within the first
few months of publication. Within a year, four more editions, in
2,000-copy print runs, were published. By 1850, approximately
30,000 copies had been published in the United States and the
British Isles, and translations had appeared in both French and
German editions.

While the *Narrative* certainly generated its share of criticism,
especially from pro-slavery advocates and Southern slaveholders,
reviews in the anti-slavery press were predictably unstinting in
their praise. A reviewer in *The Liberator* wrote that the *Narrative* 'cannot fail to produce a great sensation wherever it may
happen to circulate . . . what a lifting of the veil is this, to convince the skeptical that it is impossible to exaggerate the horrors
and enormities of that impious system!'[9] And in her review

---

[7] William Andrews rightly attributes the popularity of the 1840s fugitive slave narratives to the support and sanction of the abolitionist movement, which 'endowed slave
narratives with a moral justification similar to that which evangelicals from earlier
decades had applied' to African American spiritual autobiographies (see *To Tell a Free
Story*, 99).

[8] For a copy of Peabody's review, see William L. Andrews (ed.), *Critical Essays on
Frederick Douglass* (Boston: G. K. Hall, 1991), 24–6, reprinted from the *The Christian
Examiner*, 47 (July 1849).

[9] *The Liberator*, 23 May 1845.

published in the *New York Tribune*, Margaret Fuller, prominent journalist and feminist, rated the *Narrative* 'an excellent piece of writing', a 'specimen of the powers of the Black Race'.[10] Across the Atlantic, the *Chambers' Edinburgh Journal* praised the *Narrative* for helping to 'disseminate correct ideas respecting slavery and its attendant evils'.[11] *Littell's Living Age*, an American periodical, estimated the *Narrative*'s extensive reach: 'Taken all together, not less than one million of persons in Great Britain and Ireland have been excited by the book and its commentators.'[12]

Despite its early popularity, its commercial and critical success, the *Narrative* was out of print by the end of the 1850s, languishing from neglect until 1960, when Harvard University Press issued an edition by Benjamin Quarles, noted historian and one of Douglass's many biographers. Quarles's edition was followed in close succession by others, and the book has remained in print ever since and become the font of prodigious scholarly debate and interpretation. The varied and extensive critical commentary it has engendered illustrates that the *Narrative* is a nearly inexhaustible text. Although slight in length—numbering just over one hundred pages—the book, to borrow from Walt Whitman's 'Song of Myself', is large; it 'contains multitudes'.

What accounts for the *Narrative*'s appeal? A looming factor is the long, heroic, near epic shadow cast by 'Frederick Douglass', both the man and the mythological creation. The *Narrative* seems written with the knowledge that it was destined for History's annals; and its author, for his place among the pantheon of History's most revered and celebrated heroes. Douglass carefully crafted and recrafted his life story, making it his greatest creation, his most supreme fiction. Waldo Martin is on the mark in noting that 'Douglass carefully delineated his self-image' betraying a 'conscious and unconscious elaboration of his idealized self', and

---

[10] Margaret Fuller's review is included in Andrews and McFeeley (eds.), *Narrative of the Life*, 83.

[11] Quoted in Benjamin Quarles (ed.), *Narrative of the Life of Frederick Douglass* (Cambridge, Mass.: Harvard University Press, 1960), p. xiv.

[12] Ibid.

manifesting a 'strong compulsion to play a determinative role in the design and construction of history's heroic vision of himself'.[13]

As the 1845 *Narrative* establishes, many of these fantasies were biblical in theme, not surprising, given Douglass's extensive reading of the Bible. He pictured himself, at once, as Moses, the chosen one, masterminding his escape 'out of Egypt', and Joseph, the son sold into slavery by his brothers. The most significant events of his life are given striking biblical resonance, especially the escape attempt at Easter-time foiled by a Judas figure. In his famous fight with Covey, the overseer, he is the suffering Christ; the outcome of the fight—which transports him from bondage to freedom—is likened to the resurrection from the 'tomb' of slavery.[14] But in wrapping himself in the vestments of myth, Douglass had occluded the 'I', the personal and intimate details of his life. For example, neither his wife, Anna Murray Douglass, a free woman, who helped to finance his escape, nor their children figure in the *Narrative*.

Like so many slave narrators, Douglass's primary purpose in writing the *Narrative* was not to delineate his life story in fine detail, but rather, to advance the abolitionist cause. As Henry Louis Gates, Jr. explains, 'the black slave's narrative came to be a communal utterance, a collective tale, rather than merely an individual's autobiography. Each slave author, in writing about his or her experiences, simultaneously wrote on behalf of the millions of silent slaves still held captive throughout the South.'[15]

---

[13] Waldo E. Martin, 'The Autobiographical Douglass: Self-Made Man, Self-Concious Hero', in id., *The Mind of Frederick Douglass* (Chapel Hill: University of North Carolina Press, 1984), 273.

[14] In his excellent introduction to the Bedford edition of the *Narrative*, David Blight places the book in the tradition of the American jeremiad, a political sermon named for the book of Jeremiah. As Blight points out, 'the book is imbued with Biblical references, imagery, and metaphors, and it owes much to the black sermonic tradition from which Douglass had learned a great deal about the use of language and its powers' (*Narrative of the Life of Frederick Douglass* (Boston: Bedford Books, 1993), 8). See also Robert O'Meally's 'Frederick Douglass's 1845 *Narrative*: The Text Was Meant to be Preached', in Dexter Fisher and Robert Stepto (eds.), *Afro-American Literature: The Reconstruction of Instruction* (New York: Modern Language Association of America, 1979). O'Meally describes the *Narrative* as a 'holy book', meant, as the title suggests, to be 'mightily preached' (p. 193).

[15] Henry Louis Gates, Jr, *The Classic Slave Narratives* (New York: New American Library, 1987), p. x. Most critics agree that *My Bondage and My Freedom* is slightly more revealing—both about Douglass's life and about slave culture, than the 1845 *Narrative*.

Douglass's recognition as the 'representative' black man of the nineteenth century, as the 'voice' of the majority of 'silent' slaves, has often obscured his more complex relationship to freedom and bondage, to subjectivity and servitude. To escape bondage, to claim property in himself—to become his own 'master', as it were—was Douglass's driving ambition. Self-ownership would be the irrefutable proof of 'freedom'. Douglass was to learn, again and again, however, that self-mastery and freedom were very fluid concepts requiring constant negotiation and renegotiation, even within the context of abolitionism.

Following his escape from Maryland to Massachusetts, in his new role as abolitionist agent, Douglass was anything but 'free'. He had to struggle to wrest control and possession of himself even from the white abolitionists supposedly sworn to protect not only his newly found freedom, but also sworn to destroy the institution of slavery. Their emancipatory zeal and rhetoric not-withstanding, the abolitionists meant to claim similar, if symbolic, title in Douglass. In *My Bondage and My Freedom*, his second autobiography, Douglass effectively makes this point, summoning his characteristically mordant sarcasm to describe a typical engagement on the anti-slavery platform: 'I was generally introduced as "chattel"—a "thing"—a piece of Southern "property"—the chairman assuring the audience that *it* could speak' as a 'graduate from the peculiar institution', his 'diploma written on [his] back'.[16]

While the diploma on his back would pin Douglass in the body, reducing him to a mere physical specimen, he seized the power of the written word to redirect attention to his mind and keep it riveted there.[17] Douglass wilfully and successfully projected the voice of the learned ex-slave, defying the abolitionists who

---

[16] Frederick Douglass, *My Bondage and My Freedom*, in William L. Andrews (ed.), *The Oxford Frederick Douglass Reader* (New York: Oxford University Press, 1996), 213, 212.

[17] Karen Sanchez Eppler does well to note that 'the human body was seen to function as the foundation, not only of a general subjection, but also of a specific exclusion from political discourse'. See 'Bodily Bonds: The Intersecting Rhetorics of Feminism and Abolition', *Representations*, 24 (Fall 1988), 30. Douglass was determined to be part of that discourse and not be taken as a 'text' for abolitionists.

urged him to restore to his lectures a 'little of the plantation speech'.[18]

As some critics have observed, Douglass was removed from plantation speech, distant from the dialect of slaves, and bound inescapably to the 'master's' language, symbolically speaking. For example, Houston Baker, Jr. argues that once Douglass achieved literacy, he was necessarily distanced from the

domain of experience constituted by the oral–aural community of the slave quarters. . . . The voice of the unwritten self, once it is subjected to the linguistic codes, literary conventions, and audience expectations of a literate population, is perhaps never again the authentic voice of black American slavery. It is, rather, the voice of a self transformed by an autobiographical act into a sharer in the general public discourse about slavery.[19]

Without doubt or apology, Douglass fought not just to share in the public discourse about slavery, but to share in shaping it. Even though what he read and wrote was inevitably stamped by his white audience and sponsors, he was far from being an unwitting parrot of his sources or an exile from African-American cultural forms. Thad Ziolkowski does well to question Baker's seeming requirement that Douglass 'write as though he cannot write', for in so doing, Baker effectively inverts the 'usual hierarchy of literary values in the case of slave narratives, assigning illiteracy to the place of highest standard'.[20]

Recent scholars, such as Samira Kawash, have summoned the frequently quoted remarks of M. M. Bakhtin to describe Douglass's complicated relation to literacy and language both under the slave regime and beyond. 'Language,' Bakhtin argues, 'is not a neutral medium that passes freely and easily into the

[18] As his biographer, William McFeeley writes, 'slavery had not left [Douglass] a beast to be displayed; he was not a black dummy manipulated by a white ventriloquist' (see *Frederick Douglass* (New York: W. W. Norton, 1991), 113).

[19] Houston Baker, Jr, 'Autobiographical Acts: The Voice of the Southern Slave', in id., *The Journey Back: Issues in Black Literature and Criticism* (Chicago: University of Chicago Press, 1980), 80.

[20] See Ziolkowski's 'Antitheses: The Dialectic of Violence and Literacy in Frederick Douglass's *Narrative* of 1845', in Andrews (ed.), *Critical Essays on Frederick Douglass*, 150, 151.

private property of the speaker's intention; it is populated—over-populated—with the intentions of others. Expropriating it, forcing it to submit to one's own intentions and accents, is a difficult and complicated process.'[21] Whatever the limitations, Douglass clearly attempted to bend to his will and purpose the ideologies, language, and cultural tropes of his white readership, beginning with the language of affect and sentiment.

A large part of the *Narrative*'s achievement and appeal lies in its raw affective power. The wellspring of that power was, of course, Douglass's own life and memory, but these were fed by the values and aesthetics of sentimental fiction, to which masses of nineteenth-century readers were accustomed. Arguably, the apotheosis of sentimental narrative was Harriet Beecher Stowe's *Uncle Tom's Cabin* (1852), although Stowe's investments in 'feeling right' as a conduit of social reform pervaded mid-nineteenth-century American culture.

Douglass's *Narrative* was a book that aimed straight for the heart, the reader's feeling centre, reaching its mark more often than not. It is a book 'warm with genuine feeling', noted the reviewer in the New York *Tribune*, 10 June 1845, a point with which William Lloyd Garrison concurred. In his preface to the book, which unabashedly deployed the rhetoric of sentiment, Garrison wrote, 'He who can peruse it without a tearful eye, a heaving breast, an afflicted spirit,—without being filled with an unutterable abhorrence of slavery and all its abettors . . . must have a flinty heart' (p. 7).

In order to fuel and facilitate his revolutionary aims, Douglass summoned the moral assumptions of his audience, assumptions rooted not only in Christian texts and ethics, but also the idealization of motherhood and family. Idealized motherhood was not only a powerful moral force within the US body politic, it was also the bedrock of the country's most popular and commercially successful writing in the nineteenth century. Abolitionist

[21] See M. M. Bakhtin's 'Discourse in the Novel', trans. Caryl Emerson and Michael Holquist, in Michael Holquist (ed.), *The Dialogic Imagination* (Austin: University of Texas Press, 1981), 294. See also Lisa Sisso, ' "Writing in the Spaces Left": Literacy as a Process of Becoming in the Narratives of Frederick Douglass', *American Transcendental Quarterly*, 9 (Sept. 1995), 195–227.

rhetoric regularly exploited the cultural currency of family and motherhood in its indictments of slavery, an institution that wantonly and routinely severed slave family ties for profit. As Stephanie Smith notes, 'since antebellum culture clung to the sentimental fantasy that "mother" was an iconic index of humanity, it became a useful discursive place to attack the inhumanity of slavery'.[22]

Ante-bellum slave narratives placed extreme emphasis on the broken bonds between mother and slave, none more poignantly than Douglass in the 1845 *Narrative*. Douglass opens his narrative strategically with a description of his broken genealogy and fragile family ties. The emphasis in these early paragraphs is notably on rupture and separation:

My mother and I were separated when I was but an infant... It is a common custom, in the part of Maryland from which I ran away, to part children from their mothers at a very early age. . . . For what this separation is done, I do not know, unless it be to hinder the development of the child's affection toward its mother, and to blunt and destroy the natural affection of the mother for the child. (p. 15)

Indeed, the terse and restrained, almost childlike simplicity of the passage conveys feelings so blunted that Douglass greets news of his mother's death, in his words, 'with much the same emotions I should have probably felt at the death of a stranger' (p. 16).

As he would write in *My Bondage and My Freedom*, 'It has been a life-long, standing grief to me, that I knew so little of my mother. . . . The side view of her face is imaged on my memory, and I take few steps in life without feeling her presence; but the image is mute, and I have no striking words of her's treasured up'.[23] Each time Douglass revised his autobiography, prominent among the revisions was his embellished account of his mother.

---

[22] Stephanie Smith, *Conceived by Liberty: Maternal Figures and 19th Century American Literature* (Ithaca, NY: Cornell University Press, 1994), 125. See also Elizabeth Ammons, 'Stowe's Dream of the Mother-Savior: *Uncle Tom's Cabin* and American Women Writers before the 1920s', in Eric J. Sundquist (ed.), *New Essays on Uncle Tom's Cabin* (New York: Cambridge University Press, 1986), 155–95.

[23] Frederick Douglass, *My Bondage and My Freedom*, ed. with an introduction by Philip S. Foner (New York: Dover Publications, 1969), 57.

His descriptions evolved from the vague and fragmentary outlines of the first autobiography to a descripton in *My Bondage and My Freedom* of a woman 'ineffaceably stamped upon [his] memory' (p. 52). The most significant aspect of the shift, however, is the changing emotional tenor of his relationship to his mother. Whereas he describes his feelings towards his mother as blunted in the 1845 *Narrative*, in *My Bondage and My Freedom*, mother and son are 'very deeply attached' (p. 52). Peter Walker speculates that in these passages Douglass was desperately trying 'to grow a genealogical tree in the bitter earth of slavery'.[24] As Walker continues, however, when Douglass turned to the account of his father, the result was not expansion and embellishment but short shrift and contraction.

In the versions of his narratives, Douglass had less and less to say about his father. 'I say nothing of *father*' Douglass wrote in *My Bondage and My Freedom*, 'for he is shrouded in a mystery I have never been able to penetrate. Slavery does away with fathers as it does away with families' (p. 51) . But the fact that Douglass had less and less to say about his father in his autobiographies should not be taken to imply the father's diminished importance in Douglass's imagination. Indeed, as Walker suggests, the 'theme of a lost patrimony' runs through all of his autobiographies and his obsession with recovering it, with restoring ties to the spectral white slave master rumoured to be his father, preoccupied Douglass his entire life.[25]

II

While Douglass may have been at a loss to verify the identity of his father, he claimed symbolic 'fathers', consciously and unconsciously, throughout his life and career, alternatively embracing and repudiating what they represented, from the paternalistic abolitionists to the mythic founding fathers. At the tender age of 12, Douglass happened upon Caleb Bingham's

---

[24] Peter Walker, *Moral Choices: Memory, Desire, and Imagination in Nineteenth Century American Abolition* (Baton Rogue: Louisina State University Press, 1978), 249.
[25] Ibid.

The Columbian Orator, a collection of poems, playlets, dialogues, and patriotic speeches, which he credited with kindling in him the will to freedom. From studying this book Douglass gleaned the conventions and techniques of classical rhetoric—the periodic sentences, repetitions, puns, alliteration, apostrophes, antitheses—that account in great measure for the narrative's literary power. But Douglass gleaned more than rhetorical conventions from *The Columbian Orator*; he also gleaned the rhetoric of the 'founding fathers' of the United States.

Of all the pieces in *The Columbian Orator*, Douglass singles out two pieces for special emphasis, the dialogue between a master and his slave, in which the slave is eventually manumitted through the power of his superior reasoning, and a speech on behalf of Catholic emancipation. Just why these would become 'choice documents' is obvious: they speak to the nature and meaning of freedom. Douglass's conception of freedom, throughout the *Narrative*, fully accords with conceptions of freedom contained in American revolutionary and post-revolutionary thought. As is frequently noted, that singular and reverently quoted ideal of American revolution—that 'all men are created equal'—did not extend to the slave. More to the point, within the logic of that ideal, 'American' and 'slave' were mutually contradictory. In thus subtitling the *Narrative*, 'An American Slave', it seems clear that Douglass meant to highlight that basic contradiction.

'American' and 'Slave', writes James Olney, are 'yoked by violence together, and they present the most radical, the most aggressive, the most thoroughgoing challenge imaginable to the very idea of the American nation and to the Declaration of Independence.'[26] Echoing that founding document in the final passages of his *Narrative*, Douglass punctuates the ending with 'I subscribe myself', becoming symbolically connected to Franklin, Jefferson, and other signatories of the Declaration. 'I subscribe myself', the final words of the *Narrative*, and 'written by himself'—the tag of its bold subtitle—form, according to

[26] James Olney, 'The Founding Fathers—Frederick Douglass and Booker T. Washington', in Deborah E. McDowell and Arnold Rampersad (eds.), *Slavery and the Literary Imagination* (Baltimore: Johns Hopkins University Press, 1989), 6.

Olney, a 'completed circle enclosing and securing the narrative chiasmus of [Douglass's] life', the trajectory from bondage to freedom.[27]

Significantly, Douglass chooses to place at the centre of this journey and its narration the famous confrontation with the overseer, Edward Covey, the scene containing the memorable line: 'You have seen how a man was made a slave; you shall see how a slave was made a man.' Here too, the passage aims to underscore that 'slave' and 'man' are as mutually contradictory as 'American' and 'slave'. While Douglass wrenches both these terms from their familiar meaning centres, 'he leaves untouched', argues Samira Kawash, the 'basic structuring opposition', for 'slave and man, object and subject continue to stand as absolutely opposite . . . terms'.[28] We might add that Douglass also leaves untouched the structuring opposition: male and female, for subject and object are thoroughly and conventionally gendered throughout the *Narrative*. In other words, inasmuch as 'manhood' and 'freedom' function throughout Douglass's discourse on slavery as coincident terms, his journey from slavery to freedom leaves women in the logical position of representing the condition of slavery. Douglass's refusal to be whipped represents, not only an assertion of manhood, but the transcendence of slavery, an option his *Narrative* denies to women.

Douglass's fight with Covey is the most celebrated whipping scene of the entire book. Positioned roughly midway through the text, which pivots on this scene and constitutes the midway point between slavery and freedom, the beating scene has been anticipated for several pages before it actually occurs. Douglass represents the build-up to the fight as a symbolic attempt on Covey's part to feminize him. Threatening Douglass with another of many beatings, he

ordered me to take off my clothes. I made him no answer, but stood with my clothes on. He repeated his order. I still made him no answer,

---

[27] Ibid.

[28] Samira Kawash, *Dislocating the Color Line: Identity, Hybridity, and Singularity in African-American Literature* (Palo Alto, Calif.: Stanford University Press, 1997) 34.

nor did I move to strip myself. Upon this he rushed at me with the fierceness of a tiger, tore off my clothes, and lashed me till he had worn out his switches. (p. 59)

Douglass resolves soon after to resist these whippings, resistance he equates with seizing 'manhood' and overcoming slavery. Significantly, as a resisting slave (man), he draws blood from Covey. Thus feminizing Covey, in the process, Douglass forces him to tremble 'like a leaf' (p. 67). Douglass goes on to say, 'This battle with Mr. Covey was the turning-point in my career as a slave. It rekindled the few expiring embers of freedom, and revived within me a sense of my own manhood' (p. 68). Following his victory over Covey, in which he 'repelled by force the bloody arm of slavery,' Douglass boasts: 'I had several fights, but was never whipped' (p. 69).

As Jenny Franchot observes, Douglass 'often situated the image of the victimized—often "whipped"—female body at the emotional center of his critique of slavery'.[29] Indeed, in recounting his early years in the *Narrative*, Douglass traces his introduction to slavery to the heart-rending shrieks of his Aunt Hester as she is being beaten. He sees her 'tie[d] up to a joist and whip[ped] upon her naked back till she was literally covered with blood' (p. 18). The *Narrative* is literally populated with the whipped bodies of slave women, and in each of these scenes Douglass looks on voyeuristically in a fashion tinged with eroticism.[30] There was Mr Severe, who 'whip[ped] a woman, causing the blood to run half an hour at the time' (p. 22). There was his master, who 'tie[d] up a lame young woman, and whip[ped] her with a heavy cowskin upon her naked shoulders, causing the warm red blood to drip. . . . I have known him to tie her up early in the morning and whip her before breakfast; leave her, go to his store, return at dinner and whip her again, cutting her in the places already made raw with his cruel lash' (p. 56). There was Mr Weeden, who kept

---

[29] Jenny Franchot, 'The Punishment of Esther: Frederick Douglass and the Construction of the Feminine', in Sundquist (ed.), *Frederick Douglass*, 141.

[30] Cynthia Willett argues that, in these whipping scenes, Douglass is 'act[ing] out the unmolested desires and repressed fantasies of the slaveholders' (see *Maternal Ethics and Other Slave Moralities* (New York: Routledge, 1995), 152).

the back of a slave woman 'literally raw, made so by the lash of this merciless, *religious* wretch' (p. 72). As the *Narrative* progresses, the beatings proliferate, and the women, no longer identified by name, become absolutized as a bloody mass of naked backs.

What has been made of this recital of whippings? In a very suggestive reading, William L. Andrews argues that Douglass presents the fact of whipping in 'deliberately stylized, plainly rhetorical, recognizably artificial ways'. There is nothing masked about this presentation. On the contrary, 'Douglass's choice of repetition' is his 'chief rhetorical effect'. It constitutes his 'stylistic signature' and expresses his 'performing self'. In the whipping passages, Andrews continues, 'Douglass calls attention to himself as an unabashed artificer, a maker of forms and efforts that recontextualize brute facts according to requirements of self. The freeman requires the freedom to demonstrate the potency of his own inventiveness and the sheer potentiality of language itself for rhetorical manipulation.'[31]

Intriguing though this reading is, to explain the repetition of whippings solely in rhetorical terms and in the interest of Douglass's self-expression leads to some troubling elisions and rationalizations, perhaps the most troubling elision being the black woman's body. In other words, Douglass's 'freedom'—narrative and physical alike—depends on narrating black women's bondage. He achieves his 'stylistic signature' on the backs of black women, as it were.

Such scenes of whipping, of course, were not peculiar to Douglass's narrative. They were a staple of abolitionist literature. As Richard Brodhead observes, 'Corporal punishment has been one of the most perennially vexed of questions in American cultural history,' and it had its 'historical center of gravity in America in the antebellum decades'. Both in anti-slavery

---

[31] Andrews, *To Tell A Free Story*, 134. Valerie Smith also offers an interesting reading of the whippings, which enable the reader to 'visualize the blood that masters draw from their slaves. . . . Passages such as [Douglass's Aunt Esther's beatings] provide vivid symbols of the process of dehumanization that slaves underwent as their lifeblood was literally sapped' (see *Self-Discovery and Authority in Afro-American Narrative* (Cambridge, Mass.: Harvard University Press, 1987), 21–2).

literature and in the literature of American Gothic, what Brodhead terms the 'imagination of the lash' was pervasive.[32]

Perhaps nowhere was the 'imagination of the lash' rendered more graphically and in such concentrated form than in Timothy Dwight Weld's *American Slavery As It Is*, the compilation to which Douglass repeatedly referred in his speeches and from which he borrowed liberally as he wrote the *Narrative*. Published by the American Anti-Slavery Society in May 1839, the book was considered the most widely read and the most influential abolitionist tract to appear in the United States until Harriet Beecher Stowe's *Uncle Tom's Cabin* (1852). Described by Douglass as a 'repository of human horrors', Weld's collection teemed with stories of cruel and unusual punishment, with descriptions of beatings and floggings, of mangled flesh washed down with liquid salt or scraped with the claws of a cat.

In one piece of testimony by Angelina Grimke Weld, she describes witnessing the beating of a slave girl who was stripped naked and flogged until the gashes covering her back were so deep, Weld could 'have laid [her] whole finger in them'.[33] Readers of the *Narrative* will readily recognize the striking resemblances between Weld's passage and Douglass's affecting description of sleeping on the 'cold, damp, clay floor, with my head and feet out. My feet have been so cracked with the frost, that the pen with which I am writing might be laid in the gashes.' Interestingly, in Douglass's borrowing, the slave woman's body is elided and the instrument of the lash, transferred from the slave girl's back to Douglass's feet, transposed from a scene of sexualized violence to one of desolate privation. But perhaps the most notable shift is from a scene of flogging to a scene of writing. The whip of Weld's passage becomes the pen of Douglass's, producing a scene of Douglass's transcendence through writing at woman's expense and erasure.

---

[32] Richard Brodhead, 'Sparing the Rod: Discipline and Fiction in Antebellum America', *Representations*, 21 (Winter 1988), 67. See also David Leverenz, *Manhood and the American Renaissance* (Ithaca, NY: Cornell University Press, 1989) for a discussion of beatings in Melville's *Moby Dick* and *White Jacket*, and in *Uncle Tom's Cabin*.

[33] See Appendix I for Angelina Grimké Weld's testimony (p. 107).

III

Among the many writers who contributed to the genre of the fugitive slave narrative, Douglass is, according to Henry Louis Gates, Jr, the 'clearest example of the will to power as the will to write'. It is, however, a power and a will reserved for men. Women, especially slave women, remain trapped in the physical, in the body, excluded from language and symbolic activity. Nowhere is this more apparent than in Douglass's account of the pivotal scene in which Mrs Auld is ordered by her husband to cease teaching Frederick to read.

Mr. Auld found out what was going on, and at once forbade Mrs. Auld to instruct me further, telling her, among other things, that it was unlawful, as well as unsafe, to teach a slave to read. To use his own words . . . he said, 'If you give a nigger an inch, he will take an ell. . . . Learning would *spoil* the best nigger in the world. . . . if you teach that nigger (speaking of myself) how to read, there would be no keeping him. It would forever unfit him to be a slave. He would at once become unmanageable, and of no value to his master. As to himself, it could do him no good, but a great deal of harm. It would make him discontented and unhappy'. (p. 39)

Douglass employs here what Lillie Jugurtha aptly terms 'eye dialogue'. That is, he presents personal exchanges that have the appearance of dialogue without being dialogue. As Jugurtha notices, 'there is no second speaker here, no Lucretia Auld responding to her husband. . . . One pictures, though one does not hear, a husband and a wife talking. . . . Unobtrusively, perspectives are multiplied. Monologue functions as dialogue.'[34] Mrs Auld is exiled from the scene of language.

The troubling presence/absence of women in the 1845 *Narrative* becomes all the more puzzling, given Douglass's active and lifelong involvement in the movement for women's rights. He was the most prominent among the thirty-two men attending the first women's rights convention at Seneca Falls in July 1848. Not only

---

[34] Lillie Jugurtha, 'Point of View in the Afro-American Slave Narratives by Douglass and Pennington', in John Sekora and Darwin Turner (eds.), *The Art of Slave Narrative* (McComb, Ill.: Western Illinois University Press, 1982), 113.

did Douglass play the most significant role among the men at that convention, but he would remain devoted throughout his life to fulfilling the slogan of his newspaper, *The North Star*: 'Right is of no sex—Truth is of no color.' According to Philip Foner, Douglass chose Rochester as the paper's site largely because the city boasted an active Female Anti-Slavery Society,[35] and Julia Griffiths, an Englishwoman, helped him edit the paper and increase its circulation. At every turn in Douglass's career, women were actively involved.

Although women are largely relegated to walk-on parts in Douglass's autobiographies, he left a substantial record of speeches and editorials defending their rights.[36] His stances were uncompromising, and the note he struck in such speeches as 'Emancipation of Women', delivered at the New England Women Suffrage Association reverberated throughout his career: 'woman does not ask man for the right of suffrage That is something which man has no power to give. Rights do not have their source in the will or the grace of man'.[37] Perhaps there is no greater testament to Douglass's feminist allegiances than the fact that he died on 20 February 1895, after delivering a rousing speech at a women's rights rally.

The contradictions and disjunctions between Douglass's autobiographies and his speeches and editorials illustrate the importance of evaluating his legacy in the round and resisting the stubborn simplifications of Douglass the legend and hero. The power of the *Narrative* is rooted deeply in the power of the person and historical persona, 'Frederick Douglass,' whose presence, claims Peter Walker, has 'loomed so large and has been so compelling that he has been drafted'[38] to serve various and competing social programmes and academic agenda. To be sure, Douglass's presence has been larger than life among literary scholars and historians since the 1960s. Not surprisingly, the 1845

---

[35] See Foner's introduction to *Frederick Douglass on Women's Rights* (New York: Da Capo Press, 1992).

[36] See Appendix II for a selection of Douglass's newspaper articles (p. 119).

[37] Foner, *Douglass on Women's Rights*, 119.

[38] Walker, *Moral Choices*, 212.

Narrative forms the backbone of a series of bold claims made in
Douglass's name, perhaps none more sweeping than those put
forth by James Olney.

Olney considers the 1845 *Narrative* 'the greatest of the slave
narratives and the most completely representative'. It embodies
the most defining conventions of the form and serves as proto-
type for subsequent generations of African-American writers.
Whether individual writers were conscious of imitating Douglass
or not, Olney argues, this 'ur-Text of slavery and freedom has
informed the Afro-American literary tradition from Douglass's
time to the present'.[39]

Many might object to the ease with which Olney confers on
Douglass the status of 'founding father', and on the *Narrative*,
the status of ur-text and blueprint for Olney's noticeably male
canon—Booker T. Washington, W. E. B. DuBois, and James
Weldon Johnson down to Richard Wright, Malcolm X, Ralph
Ellison, and beyond—but few would dispute that the book has
earned distinction as a 'classic' of world literature.

'Classics', we are now wont to argue, are not born but made,
and the interpretative history of the *Narrative* amply reinforces
this axiom. Although in his 1977 essay, 'Animal Farm Unbound',
H. Bruce Franklin could list in a fairly short paragraph critical
articles on the 1845 *Narrative*, now, two decades later, the book
has stimulated a small industry of scholarship that shows no signs
of abating.[40]

Critical interpretations of the *Narrative* have been as protean
as they have been voluminous. The book has adapted nimbly to
changing critical moments, fashions, and vocabularies of literary
scholarship. To offer but a thumbnail sketch of recent trends,
the *Narrative* was taken up in the 1960s and 1970s by black
nationalists in search of a 'usable' past and ancestors worthy

---

[39] Olney 'Founding Fathers', 8.

[40] For a bibliographic essay on the various editions of the Douglass narrative as
compared to other slave narratives, see Ruth Miller and Peter Katopes, 'Slave Narra-
tives' and W. Burghardt Turner, 'The Polemicists: David Walker, Frederick Douglass,
Booker T. Washington, and W. E. B. DuBois', in M. Thomas Inge, Maurice Duke, and
Jackson Bryer (eds.), *Black American Writers: Bibliographical Essays*, i (New York: St
Martins Press, 1978).

to be called revolutionaries. When revisionist historians sought to debunk the 'Sambo thesis' of Stanley Elkins's *Slavery: A Problem in American Institutional Life* (1959), Douglass's *Narrative* again proved useful. While Elkins had argued that slavery had completely emasculated the black male slave, rendering him 'half-man', 'half-child', historians, armed with a mountain of supporting data, came forth to refute Elkins's thesis. What more resounding refutation was there than Frederick Douglass, a 'man' once made a slave, who metamorphosed, through the force of his own will and power, into a whole man again. When literary Marxists turned their attention to the economics of slavery, which reduced slaves to labouring chattel, Douglass's *Narrative* easily lent itself to discussions of surplus value, exchange value, use value, commodity production, consumption, and stolen profits. Finally, the *Narrative* seemed tailor-made for academic feminists who emerged in the 1970s and 1980s to decry Douglass's investment in patriarchal privilege and ideologies of masculinity. The text has seemingly epic proportions, a term frequently invoked in discussions of Frederick Douglass and his work.

In a foreword to the 1941 edition of *Life and Times of Frederick Douglass*, the last of Douglass's three autobiographies, Alain Locke submitted that 'in the lengthening perspective of the [African-American's] history in America, the career and character of Frederick Douglass take on more and more the stature and significance of the epical'. Douglass's 'heroic cast', Locke continued, made his story an 'imperishable part of the Negro epic' and, his *Life and Times*, 'the classic of American Negro biography'. The weight of the scholarly literature, barely outlined above, poses a resounding challenge to Locke's claims for the 'classic' importance of *Life and Times*. It seems that the 1845 *Narrative* has been installed securely in that place.

NOTE ON THE TEXT

The first edition of *Narrative of the Life of Frederick Douglass, an American Slave, Written by Himself*, reprinted here, was published in May 1845 by the Anti-Slavery Office in Boston, Massachusetts.

SELECT BIBLIOGRAPHY

Biography

Graham, Shirley, *There Was Once a Slave: The Heroic Story of Frederick Douglass* (New York, 1947).

McFeeley, William S., *Frederick Douglass* (New York: W. W. Norton, 1991).

Preston, Dickson J., *Young Frederick Douglass: The Maryland Years* (Baltimore: Johns Hopkins University Press, 1980).

Quarles, Benjamin, *Frederick Douglass* (1948, repr. New York, 1968).

Critical Studies and Essays

Andrews, William, *To Tell a Free Story: The First Century of Afro-American Autobiography; 1760–1865* (Champaign: University of Illinois Press, 1986).

—— (ed.), *Critical Essays on Frederick Douglass* (Boston: G. K. Hall, 1991).

Baker, Jr, Houston, *The Journey Back: Issues in Black Literature and Criticism* (Chicago: University of Chicago Press, 1980).

—— 'Figurations for a New American Literary History: Archaeology, Ideology, and Afro-American Discourse', in *Blues, Ideology, and Afro-American Literature: A Vernacular Theory* (Chicago: University of Chicago Press, 1984), 39–49.

Blight, David, 'Introduction' to *Narrative of the Life of Frederick Douglass* (New York: Bedford Books, 1993).

Brodhead, Richard, 'Sparing the Rod: Discipline and Fiction in Antebellum America', *Representations*, 21 (Winter 1988), 67–96.

Davis, Charles T. and Gates, Jr, Henry Louis, *The Slave's Narrative* (New York: Oxford University Press, 1985).

Franchot, Jenny, 'The Punishment of Esther: Frederick Douglass and the Construction of the Feminine', in Eric J. Sundquist (ed.), *Frederick Douglass: New Literary and Historical Essays* (New York: Cambridge University Press, 1990).

Gates, Jr, Henry Louis, 'Frederick Douglass and the Language of the Self', in *Figures in Black: Words, Signs, and the 'Racial' Self* (New York: Oxford University Press, 1987), 98–124.

Kawash, Samira, *Dislocating the Color Line: Identity, Hybridity, and Singularity in African-American Literature* (Palo Alto, Calif.: Stanford University Press, 1997).

McDowell, Deborah E., 'In the First Place: Making Frederick and the Afro-American Narrative Tradition', in William Andrews (ed.), *Critical Essays on Frederick Douglass* (Boston: G. K. Hall, 1991), 192–214.

Martin, Waldo E., *The Mind of Frederick Douglass* (Chapel Hill: University of North Carolina Press, 1984).

Olney, James, 'The Founding Fathers—Frederick Douglass and Booker T. Washington', in Deborah E. McDowell and Arnold Rampersad (eds.), *Slavery and the Literary Imagination* (Baltimore: John Hopkins University Press, 1989), 1–24.

O'Meally, Robert, 'The Text Was Meant to Be Preached', in Dexter Fisher and Robert Stepto (eds.), *Afro-American Literature: The Reconstruction of Instruction* (New York: Modern Language Association, 1979), 192–211.

Sanchez-Eppler, Karen, 'Bodily Bonds: The Intersecting Rhetorics of Feminism and Abolition', *Representations*, 24 (Fall 1988), 28–60.

Sisco, Lisa, ' "Writing in the Spaces Left": Literacy as Process of Becoming in the Narratives of Frederick Douglass', *American Transcendental Quarterly*, 9 (Sept. 1995), 195–227.

Smith, Cynthia, 'Frederick Douglass's Strategic Sentimentality', in *Conceived by Liberty: Maternal Figures and 19th Century American Literature* (Ithaca, NY: Cornell University Press, 1994).

Smith, Valerie, *Self-Discovery and Authority in Afro-American Narrative* (Cambridge, Mass.: Harvard University Press, 1987).

Stepto, Robert, *From Behind the Veil: A Study of Afro-American Narrative* (Urbana: University of Illinois Press, 1979), 32–51.

Sundquist, Eric, 'Frederick Douglass: Literacy and Paternalism', *Raritan*, 6 (Fall 1986), 108–24.

Walker, Peter, *Moral Choices: Memory, Desire, and Imagination in Nineteenth Century American Abolition* (Baton Rouge: Louisiana State University Press, 1978).

Further Reading in Oxford World's Classics

Crèvecœur, J. Hector St John, 'Description of Charles-Town; Thoughts on Slavery ...', in *Letters from an American Farmer*, ed. Susan Manning.

Stowe, Harriet Beecher, *Uncle Tom's Cabin*, ed. Jean Fagan Yellin.

Washington, Booker T., *Up From Slavery*, ed. William L. Andrews.

A CHRONOLOGY OF FREDERICK DOUGLASS

1818   Frederick Augustus Washington Bailey is born in February at Holme Hill Farm, in Talbot County on the Eastern Shore of Maryland, the son of Harriet Bailey, a slave, and an unknown white man.

1825   Harriet Bailey dies.

1826   Douglass is sent to live with Hugh and Sophia Auld in Baltimore. Receives initial reading lessons from Sophia Auld. Works as family servant and errand boy.

1833   Returned to his master, Thomas Auld, in St Michaels, Talbot County, Maryland.

1834   Hired for a year to Edward Covey, a local farmer known for his skill in 'breaking' recalcitrant slaves. In August, Douglass reaches a turning-point in his slave career after successfully resisting a Covey beating.

1836   Returned to Baltimore to learn the caulking trade.

1838   Escapes slavery on 3 September with the aid of borrowed American merchantman seaman's papers and money from his fiancée, Anna Murray, a free black woman of Baltimore. Marries Anna on 15 September in New York. Moves to New Bedford, Massachusetts, changes his name to Frederick Douglass, and finds work as a general labourer.

1839   Licensed to preach by the New Bedford African Methodist Episcopal Zion Church.

1841   Becomes a salaried lecturer for the Massachusetts Anti-Slavery Society. Travels throughout New England recounting his experiences as a slave. Staunchly advocates William Lloyd Garrison's brand of non-violent, non-political agitation against slavery.

1845   *Narrative of the Life of Frederick Douglass, an American Slave. Written by Himself* is published by the Anti-Slavery office in Boston. Douglass goes on extended speaking tour of Great Britain.

1847   Freedom purchased by British friends. Returns to the United States, moves to Rochester, New York, and launches his own anti-slavery weekly, *The North Star*.

1848   Attends Seneca Falls Woman's Rights Convention. Publishes 'To My Old Master, Thomas Auld' in *The North Star*.

1851   Breaks with Garrison over anti-slavery strategy. Starts *Frederick Douglass' Paper* with financial support of Gerrit Smith, a New York abolitionist.

1852   Delivers famous address, 'What to the Slave is the Fourth of July?' in Rochester, later published as a pamphlet.

1853   *The Heroic Slave* published in *Autographs for Freedom*, edited by Douglass's friend and adviser, Julia Griffiths.

1855   *My Bondage and My Freedom* is published by Miller, Orton, and Mulligan in New York.

1859   Begins *Douglass' Monthly*. Discusses with John Brown the latter's plan to arm a guerrilla army at Harper's Ferry to help Virginia slaves escape. Opposes the plan. Flees to Canada after warrant is issued for his arrest as an accomplice in Brown's raid on the arsenal at Harper's Ferry, Virginia.

1860   Death of daughter Annie. Supports Abraham Lincoln for president of the United States.

1861   Welcomes the outbreak of the Civil War. Lobbies Lincoln to allow black men to enter the Union Army.

1863   Becomes recruiting agent for the 54th Massachusetts Infantry regiment, in which sons Charles Remond Douglass and Lewis Henry Douglass serve. Ceases publishing *Douglass' Monthly*.

1864   Works for Lincoln's re-election and for prosecution of the war until slavery is extirpated.

1866   Criticizes Reconstruction policies of President Andrew Johnson; advocates black suffrage in the South. Begins career as a lyceum lecturer on a variety of topics, the most widely requested of which is 'Self-Made Men'.

1868   Attacked by friends in the feminist movement for placing a higher priority on black manhood suffrage than on women's suffrage.

1870   Moves to Washington, DC to become editor-in-chief of *The New National Era*, a reformist weekly.

1871   Appointed by President Ulysses S. Grant to serve as assistant secretary to a commission considering possible annexation of the Dominican Republic. Recommends annexation in *New National Era*.

1872   Campaigns for Grant. House in Rochester destroyed by fire.

1874   Named president of the Freedman's Savings and Trust Company; bank fails within a few months. Loses substantial investments in its collapse and in the closing of *The New National Era*.

1877   Appointed US Marshall for District of Columbia by President Rutherford B. Hayes. Returns to St Michaels to visit relatives and former master, Hugh Auld.

1878   Moves to Cedar Hill estate in Anacostia, District of Columbia.

1879   Criticized because of his public censure of the Exoduster migration from the South to Kansas.

1881   Appointed Recorder of Deeds for the District of Columbia. *Life and Times of Frederick Douglass* published by the Park publishing company of Hartford, Connecticut.

1882   Death of Anna Murray Douglass.

1883   Increasingly disenchanted with national government's failure to protect African-American civil rights in the South.

1884   Marries Helen Pitts, a white woman active in women's rights work. Condemned by many blacks and whites alike for interracial marriage.

1886–7 Tours Europe and Egypt with Helen Douglass.

1889   Appointed Minister and Consul General to Haiti by President Benjamin Harrison.

1891   Resigns as Minister to Haiti after breakdown of negotiations for leasing of the port at Mole St Nicolas.

1892   Expanded edition of *Life and Times of Frederick Douglass* published by De Wolfe, Fiske, and Company of Boston.

1893   Introduces Ida B. Wells's pamphlet *The Reason Why the Colored American Is Not in the World Columbian Exposition* in Chicago.

1894   *The Lessons of the Hour*, a denunciation of lynching, published as a pamphlet in Baltimore, Maryland.

1895   Dies at Cedar Hill on 20 February after addressing the National Council of Women. Buried 26 February in Rochester's Mount Hope Cemetery.

NARRATIVE OF
THE LIFE OF
FREDERICK DOUGLASS,
AN AMERICAN SLAVE,
WRITTEN BY HIMSELF

PREFACE*

In the month of August, 1841, I attended an anti-slavery convention in Nantucket, at which it was my happiness to become acquainted with FREDERICK DOUGLASS, the writer of the following Narrative. He was a stranger to nearly every member of that body; but, having recently made his escape from the southern prison-house of bondage, and feeling his curiosity excited to ascertain the principles and measures of the abolitionists,—of whom he had heard a somewhat vague description while he was a slave,—he was induced to give his attendance, on the occasion alluded to, though at that time a resident of New Bedford.*

Fortunate, most fortunate occurrence!—fortunate for the millions of his manacled brethren, yet panting for deliverance from their awful thraldom!—fortunate for the cause of negro emancipation, and of universal liberty!*—fortunate for the land of his birth, which he has already done so much to save and bless!—fortunate for a large circle of friends and acquaintances, whose sympathy and affection he has strongly secured by the many sufferings he has endured, by his virtuous traits of character, by his ever-abiding remembrance of those who are in bonds, as being bound with them!—fortunate for the multitudes, in various parts of our republic, whose minds he has enlightened on the subject of slavery, and who have been melted to tears by his pathos, or roused to virtuous indignation by his stirring eloquence against the enslavers of men!—fortunate for himself, as it at once brought him into the field of public usefulness, "gave the world assurance of a MAN,"* quickened the slumbering energies of his soul, and consecrated him to the great work of breaking the rod of the oppressor, and letting the oppressed go free!

I shall never forget his first speech at the convention—the extraordinary emotion it excited in my own mind—the powerful impression it created upon a crowded auditory, completely taken by surprise—the applause which followed from the beginning to the end of his felicitous remarks. I think I never hated slavery so intensely as at that moment; certainly, my perception of the enormous outrage which is inflicted by it, on the godlike nature of its victims, was rendered far more clear than ever. There stood one, in physical proportion and stature commanding and exact—in intellect richly endowed—in natural eloquence a prodigy—in soul manifestly "created but a little lower than the angels"*—yet a slave, ay, a fugitive slave,—trembling for his safety, hardly daring to believe that on the American soil, a single white person could be found who would befriend him at all hazards, for the love of God and humanity! Capable of high attainments as an intellectual and moral being—needing nothing but a comparatively small amount of cultivation to make him an ornament to society and a blessing to his race—by the law of the land, by the voice of the people, by the terms of the slave code, he was only a piece of property, a beast of burden, a chattel personal, nevertheless!

A beloved friend* from New Bedford prevailed on Mr. DOUGLASS to address the convention. He came forward to the platform with a hesitancy and embarrassment, necessarily the attendants of a sensitive mind in such a novel position. After apologizing for his ignorance, and reminding the audience that slavery was a poor school for the human intellect and heart, he proceeded to narrate some of the facts in his own history as a slave, and in the course of his speech gave utterance to many noble thoughts and thrilling reflections. As soon as he had taken his seat, filled with hope and admiration, I rose, and declared that PATRICK HENRY,* of revolutionary fame, never made a speech more eloquent in the cause of liberty, than the one we had just listened to from the lips of that hunted fugitive. So I believed at that time—such is my belief now. I reminded the audience of the peril which surrounded this self-emancipated young man at the North,—even in Massachusetts, on the soil of the Pilgrim Fathers, among the descendants of revolutionary sires; and I appealed to them, whether they would ever allow him to be carried back into slavery,—law or no law, constitution or no constitution. The response was unanimous and in thunder-tones— "NO!" "Will you succor and protect him as a brother-man—a resident of the old Bay State?"* "YES!" shouted the whole mass, with an energy so startling, that the ruthless tyrants south of Mason and Dixon's line might almost have heard the mighty burst of feeling, and recognized it as the pledge of an invincible determination, on the part of those who gave it, never to betray him that wanders, but to hide the outcast, and firmly to abide the consequences.

It was at once deeply impressed upon my mind, that, if Mr. DOUGLASS could be persuaded to consecrate his time and talents to the promotion of the anti-slavery enterprise, a powerful impetus would be given to it, and a stunning blow at the same time inflicted on northern prejudice* against a colored complexion. I therefore endeavored to instil hope and courage into his mind, in order that he might dare to engage in a vocation so anomalous and responsible for a person in his situation; and I was seconded in this effort by warm-hearted friends, especially by the late General Agent of the Massachusetts Anti-Slavery Society, Mr. JOHN A. COLLINS,* whose judgment in this instance entirely coincided with my own. At first, he could give no encouragement; with unfeigned diffidence, he expressed his conviction that he was not adequate to the performance of so great a task; the path marked out was wholly an untrodden one; he was sincerely apprehensive that he should do more harm than good. After much deliberation, however, he consented to make a trial; and ever since that period, he has acted as a lecturing agent, under the auspices either of the American or the Massachusetts Anti-Slavery Society. In labors he has been most abundant; and his success in combating prejudice, in gaining proselytes, in agitating the public mind, has far surpassed the most sanguine expectations that were raised at the commencement of his brilliant career. He has borne himself with gentleness and meekness, yet with true manliness of character. As a public speaker, he excels in pathos, wit, comparison, imitation, strength of reasoning, and fluency of language. There is in him that union of head and heart, which is indispensable to an enlightenment of the heads and a winning of the hearts of others. May his strength continue to be equal to his day! May he continue to "grow in grace, and in the knowledge of God,"* that he may be increasingly serviceable in the cause of bleeding humanity, whether at home or abroad!

It is certainly a very remarkable fact, that one of the most efficient advocates of the slave population, now before the public, is a fugitive slave, in the person of FREDERICK DOUGLASS; and that the free colored population of the United States are as ably represented by one of their own number, in the person of CHARLES LENOX REMOND,* whose eloquent appeals have extorted the highest applause of multitudes on both sides of the Atlantic. Let the calumniators of the colored race despise themselves for their baseness and illiberality of spirit, and henceforth cease to talk of the natural inferiority of those who require nothing but time and opportunity to attain to the highest point of human excellence.

It may, perhaps, be fairly questioned, whether any other portion of the population of the earth could have endured the privations, sufferings and horrors of slavery, without having become more degraded in the scale of humanity than the slaves of African descent. Nothing has been left undone to cripple their intellects, darken their minds, debase their moral nature, obliterate all traces of their relationship to mankind; and yet how wonderfully they have sustained the might load of a most frightful bondage, under which they have been groaning for centuries! To illustrate the effect of slavery on the white man,—to show that he has no powers of endurance, in such a condition, superior to those of his black brother,—DANIEL O'CONNELL,* the distinguished advocate of universal emancipation, and the mightiest champion of prostrate but not conquered Ireland, relates the following anecdote in a speech delivered by him in the Conciliation Hall, Dublin, before the Loyal National Repeal Association,* March 31, 1845. "No matter," said Mr. O'CONNELL, "under what specious term it may disguise itself, slavery is still hideous. *It has a natural, an inevitable tendency to brutalize every noble faculty of man.* An American sailor, who was cast away on the shore of Africa, where he was kept in slavery for three years, was, at the expiration of that period, found to be imbruted and stultified— he had lost all reasoning power; and having forgotten his native language, could only utter some savage gibberish between Arabic and English, which nobody could understand, and which even he himself found difficulty in pronouncing. So much for the humanizing influence of THE DOMESTIC INSTITUTION!" Admitting this to have been an extraordinary case of mental deterioration, it proves at least that the white slave can sink as low in the scale of humanity as the black one.

Mr. DOUGLASS has very properly chosen to write his own Narrative, in his own style, and according to the best of his ability, rather than to employ some one else. It is, therefore, entirely his own production; and, considering how long and dark was the career he had to run as a slave,—how few have been his opportunities to improve his mind since he broke his iron fetters,—it is, in my judgment, highly creditable to his head and heart. He who can peruse it without a tearful eye, a heaving breast, an afflicted spirit,—without being filled with an unutterable abhorrence of slavery and all its abettors, and animated with a determination to seek the immediate overthrow of that execrable system,—without trembling for the fate of this country in the hands of a righteous God, who is ever on the side of the oppressed, and whose arm is not shortened that it cannot save,—must have a flinty heart, and be qualified to act the part of a trafficker "in slaves and the souls of men."* I am confident that it is essentially true in all its statements; that nothing has been set down in malice, nothing exaggerated, nothing drawn from the imagination; that it comes short of the reality, rather than overstates a single fact in regard to SLAVERY AS IT IS. The experience of FREDERICK DOUGLASS, as a slave, was not a peculiar one; his lot was not especially a hard one; his case may be regarded as a very fair specimen of the treatment of slaves in Maryland, in which State it is conceded that they are better fed and less cruelly treated than in Georgia, Alabama, or Louisiana. Many have suffered incomparably more, while very few on the plantations have suffered less, than himself. Yet how deplorable was his situation! what terrible chastisements were inflicted upon his person! what still more shocking outrages were perpetrated upon his mind! with all his noble powers and sublime aspirations, how like a brute was he treated, even by those professing to have the same mind in them that was in Christ Jesus! to what dreadful liabilities was he continually subjected! how destitute of friendly counsel and aid, even in his greatest extremities! how heavy was the midnight of woe which shrouded in blackness the last ray of hope, and filled the future with terror and gloom! what longings after freedom took possession of his breast, and how his misery augmented, in proportion as he grew reflective and intelligent,—thus demonstrating that a happy slave is an extinct man! how he thought, reasoned, felt, under the lash of the driver, with the chains upon his limbs! what perils he encountered in his endeavors to escape from his horrible doom! and how signal have been his deliverance and preservation in the midst of a nation of pitiless enemies!

This Narrative contains many affecting incidents, many passages of great eloquence and power; but I think the most thrilling one of them all is the description DOUGLASS gives of his feelings, as he stood soliloquizing respecting his fate, and the chances of his one day being a freeman, on the banks of the Chesapeake Bay—viewing the receding vessels as they flew with their white wings before the breeze, and apostrophizing them as animated by the living spirit of freedom. Who can read that passage, and be insensible to its pathos and sublimity? Compressed into it is a whole Alexandrian library* of thought, feeling, and sentiment— all that can, all that need be urged, in the form of expostulation, entreaty, rebuke, against that crime of crimes,—making man the property of his fellow-man! O, how accursed is that system, which entombs the godlike mind of man, defaces the divine image, reduces those who by creation were crowned with glory and honor to a level with four-footed beasts, and exalts the dealer in human flesh above all that is called God! Why should its existence be prolonged one hour? Is it not evil, only evil, and that continually? What does its presence imply but the absence of all fear of God, all regard for man, on the part of the people of the United States? Heaven speed its eternal overthrow!

So profoundly ignorant of the nature of slavery are many persons, that they are stubbornly incredulous whenever they read or listen to any recital of the cruelties which are daily inflicted on its victims. They do not deny that the slaves are held as property; but that terrible fact seems to convey to their minds no idea of injustice, exposure to outrage, or savage barbarity. Tell them of cruel scourgings, of mutilations and brandings, of scenes of pollution and blood, of the banishment of all light and knowledge, and they affect to be greatly indignant at such enormous exaggerations, such wholesale misstatements, such abominable libels on the character of the southern planters! As if all these direful outrages were not the natural results of slavery! As if it were less cruel to reduce a human being to the condition of a thing, than to give him a severe flagellation, or to deprive him of necessary food and clothing! As if whips, chains, thumb-screws, paddles, bloodhounds, overseers, drivers, patrols, were not all indispensable to keep the slaves down, and to give protection to their ruthless oppressors! As if, when the marriage institution is abolished, concubinage, adultery, and incest, must not necessarily abound; when all the rights of humanity are annihilated, any barrier remains to protect the victim from the fury of the spoiler; when absolute power is assumed over life and liberty, it will not be wielded with destructive sway! Skeptics of this character abound in society. In some few instances, their incredulity arises from a want of reflection; but, generally, it indicates a hatred of the light, a desire to shield slavery from the assaults of its foes, a contempt of the colored race, whether bond or free. Such will try to discredit the shocking tales of slaveholding cruelty which are recorded in this truthful Narrative; but they will labor in vain. Mr. DOUGLASS has frankly disclosed the place of his birth, the names of those who claimed ownership in his body and soul, and the names also of those who committed the crimes which he has alleged against them. His statements, therefore, may easily be disproved, if they are untrue.

In the course of his Narrative, he relates two instances of murderous cruelty,—in one of which a planter deliberately shot a slave belonging to a neighboring plantation, who had unintentionally gotten within his lordly domain in quest of fish; and in the other, an overseer blew out the brains of a slave who had fled to a stream of water to escape a bloody scourging.

Mr. DOUGLASS states that in neither of these instances was any thing done by way of legal arrest or judicial investigation. The Baltimore American, of March 17, 1845, relates a similar case of atrocity, perpetrated with similar impunity—as follows:— "*Shooting a Slave.*—We learn, upon the authority of a letter from Charles country, Maryland, received by a gentleman of this city, that a young man, named Matthews, a nephew of General Matthews, and whose father, it is believed, holds an office at Washington, killed one of the slaves upon his father's farm by shooting him. The letter states that young Matthews had been left in charge of the farm; that he gave an order to the servant, which was disobeyed, when he proceeded to the house, *obtained a gun, and, returning, shot the servant*. He immediately, the letter continues, fled to his father's residence, where he still remains unmolested."—Let it never be forgotten, that no slaveholder or overseer can be convicted of any outrage perpetrated on the person of a slave, however diabolical it may be, on the testimony of colored witnesses, whether bond or free. By the slave code,* they are adjudged to be as incompetent to testify against a white man, as though they were indeed a part of the brute creation. Hence, there is no legal protection in fact, whatever there may be in form, for the slave population; and any amount of cruelty may be inflicted on them with impunity. Is it possible for the human mind to conceive of a more horrible state of society?

The effect of a religious profession on the conduct of southern masters is vividly described in the following Narrative, and shown to be any thing but salutary. In the nature of the case, it must be in the highest degree pernicious. The testimony of Mr. DOUGLASS, on this point, is sustained by a cloud of witnesses, whose veracity is unimpeachable. "A slaveholder's profession of Christianity is a palpable imposture. He is a felon of the highest grade. He is a man-stealer. It is of no importance what you put in the other scale."

Reader! are you with the man-stealers in sympathy and purpose, or on the side of their down-trodden victims? If with the former, then are you the foe of God and man. If with the latter, what are you prepared to do and dare in their behalf? Be faithful, be vigilant, be untiring in your efforts to break every yoke, and let the oppressed go free. Come what may—cost what it may—inscribe on the banner which you unfurl to the breeze, as your religious and political motto—"NO COMPROMISE WITH SLAVERY! NO UNION WITH SLAVEHOLDERS!"*

WM. LLOYD GARRISON

Boston, *May* 1, 1845

LETTER FROM WENDELL PHILLIPS, ESQ.*

Boston, *April* 22, 1845

My Dear Friend:

YOU remember the old fable of "The Man and the Lion," where the lion complained that he should not be so misrepresented "when the lions wrote history."

I am glad the time has come when the "lions write history." We have been left long enough to gather the character of slavery from the involuntary evidence of the masters. One might, indeed, rest sufficiently satisfied with what, it is evident, must be, in general, the results of such a relation, without seeking farther to find whether they have followed in every instance. Indeed, those who stare at the half-peck of corn a week, and love to count the lashes on the slave's back, are seldom the "stuff" out of which reformers and abolitionists are to be made. I remember that, in 1838, many were waiting for the results of the West India experiment,* before they could come into our ranks. Those "results" have come long ago; but, alas! few of that number have come with them, as converts. A man must be disposed to judge of emancipation by other tests than whether it has increased the produce of sugar,—and to hate slavery for other reasons than because it starves men and whips women,—before he is ready to lay the first stone of his anti-slavery life.

I was glad to learn, in your story, how early the most neglected of God's children waken to a sense of their rights, and of the injustice done them. Experience is a keen teacher; and long before you had mastered your A B C, or knew where the "white sails" of the Chesapeake were bound, you began, I see, to gauge the wretchedness of the slave, not by his hunger and want, not by his lashes and toil, but by the cruel and blighting death which gathers over his soul.

In connection with this, there is one circumstance which makes your recollections peculiarly valuable, and renders your early insight the more remarkable. You come from that part of the country where we are told slavery appears with its fairest features. Let us hear, then, what it is at its best estate—gaze on its bright side, if it has one; and then imagination may task her powers to add dark lines to the picture, as she travels southward to that (for the colored man) Valley of the Shadow of Death, where the Mississippi sweeps along.

Again, we have known you long, and can put the most entire confidence in your truth, candor, and sincerity. Every one who has heard you speak has felt, and, I am confident, every one who reads your book will feel, persuaded that you give them a fair specimen of the whole truth. No one-sided portrait,—no wholesale complaints,—but strict justice done, whenever individual kindliness has neutralized, for a moment, the deadly system with which it was strangely allied. You have been with us, too, some years, and can fairly compare the twilight of rights, which your race enjoy at the North with that "noon of night"* under which they labor south of Mason and Dixon's line. Tell us whether, after all, the half-free colored man of Massachusetts is worse off than the pampered slave of the rice swamps!

In reading your life, no one can say that we have unfairly picked out some rare specimens of cruelty. We know that the bitter drops, which even you have drained from the cup, are no incidental aggravations, no individual ills, but such as must mingle always and necessarily in the lot of every slave. They are the essential ingredients, not the occasional results, of the system.

After all, I shall read your book with trembling for you. Some years ago, when you were beginning to tell me your real name and birthplace, you may remember I stopped you, and preferred to remain ignorant of all. With the exception of a vague description, so I continued, till the other day, when you read me your memoirs. I hardly knew, at the time, whether to thank you or not for the sight of them, when I reflected that it was still dangerous, in Massachusetts, for honest men to tell their names! They say the fathers, in 1776, signed the Declaration of Independence with the halter about their necks. You, too, publish your declaration of freedom with danger compassing you around. In all the broad lands which the Constitution of the United States overshadows, there is no single spot,—however narrow or desolate,— where a fugitive slave can plant himself and say, "I am safe." The whole armory of Northern Law has no shield for you. I am free to say that, in your place, I should throw the MS. into the fire.

You, perhaps, may tell your story in safety, endeared as you are to so many warm hearts by rare gifts, and a still rarer devotion of them to the service of others. But it will be owing only to your labor, and the fearless efforts of those who, trampling the laws and Constitution of the country under their feet, are determined that they will "hide the outcast,"* and that their hearths shall be, spite of the law, an asylum for the oppressed, if, some time or other, the humblest may stand in our streets, and bear witness in safety against the cruelties of which he has been the victim.

Yet it is sad to think, that these very throbbing hearts which welcome your story, and from your best safeguard in telling it, are all beating contrary to the "statute in such case made and provided." Go on, my dear friend, till you, and those who, like you, have been saved, so as by fire, from the dark prison-house, shall stereotype these free, illegal pulses into statutes; and New England, cutting loose from a blood-stained Union, shall glory in being the house of refuge for the oppressed;—till we no longer merely "*hide* the outcast," or make a merit of standing idly by while he is hunted in our midst; but, consecrating anew the soil of the Pilgrims as an asylum for the oppressed, proclaim our *welcome* to the slave so loudly, that the tones shall reach every hut in the Carolinas, and make the broken-hearted bondman leap up at the thought of old Massachusetts.

> God speed the day!
> Till then, and ever,
> Yours truly,
> WENDELL PHILLIPS

CHAPTER I

I was born in Tuckahoe, near Hillsborough, and about twelve miles from Easton, in Talbot county, Maryland. I have no accurate knowledge of my age, never having seen any authentic record containing it. By far the larger part of the slaves know as little of their ages as horses know of theirs, and it is the wish of most masters within my knowledge to keep their slaves thus ignorant. I do not remember to have ever met a slave who could tell of his birthday. They seldom come nearer to it than planting-time, harvest-time, cherry-time, spring-time, or fall-time. A want of information concerning my own was a source of unhappiness to me even during childhood. The white children could tell their ages. I could not tell why I ought to be deprived of the same privilege. I was not allowed to make any inquiries of my master concerning it. He deemed all such inquiries on the part of a slave improper and impertinent, and evidence of a restless spirit. The nearest estimate I can give makes me now between twenty–seven and twenty–eight years of age. I come to this, from hearing my master say, some time during 1835, I was about seventeen years old.*

My mother was named Harriet Bailey. She was the daughter of Isaac and Betsey Bailey, both colored, and quite dark. My mother was of a darker complexion than either my grandmother or grandfather.

My father was a white man. He was admitted to be such by all I ever heard speak of my parentage. The opinion was also whispered that my master was my father; but of the correctness of this opinion, I know nothing; the means of knowing was withheld from me. My mother and I were separated when I was but an infant—before I knew her as my mother. It is a common custom, in the part of Maryland from which I ran away, to part children from their mothers at a very early age. Frequently, before the child has reached its twelfth month, its mother is taken from it, and hired out on some farm a considerable distance off, and the child is placed under the care of an old woman, too old for field labor. For what this separation is done, I do not know, unless it be to hinder the development of the child's affection toward its mother, and to blunt and destroy the natural affection of the mother for the child. This is the inevitable result.

I never saw my mother, to know her as such, more than four or five times in my life; and each of these times was very short in duration, and at night. She was hired by a Mr. Stewart, who lived about twelve miles from my home. She made her journeys to see me in the night, travelling the whole distance on foot, after the performance of her day's work. She was a field hand, and a whipping is the penalty of not being in the field at sunrise, unless a slave has special permission from his or her master to the contrary—a permission which they seldom get, and one that gives to him that gives it the proud name of being a kind master. I do not recollect of ever seeing my mother by the light of day. She was with me in the night. She would lie down with me, and get me to sleep, but long before I waked she was gone. Very little communication ever took place between us. Death soon ended what little we could have while she lived, and with it her hardships and suffering. She died when I was about seven years old, on one of my master's farms, near Lee's Mill. I was not allowed to be present during her illness, at her death, or burial. She was gone long before I knew any thing about it. Never having enjoyed, to any considerable extent, her soothing presence, her tender and watchful care, I received the tidings of her death with much the same emotions I should have probably felt at the death of a stranger.

Called thus suddenly away, she left me without the slightest intimation of who my father was. The whisper that my master was my father, may or may not be true; and, true or false, it is of but little consequence to my purpose whilst the face remains, in all its glaring odiousness, that slaveholders have ordained, and by law established, that the children of slave women shall in all cases follow the condition of their mothers; and this is done too obviously to administer to their own lusts, and make gratification of their wicked desires profitable as well as pleasurable; for by this cunning arrangement, the slaveholder, in cases not a few, sustains to his slaves the double relation of master and father.

I know of such cases; and it is worthy of remark that such slaves invariably suffer greater hardships, and have more to contend with, than others. They are, in the first place, a constant offence to their mistress. She is ever disposed to find fault with them; they can seldom do any thing to please her; she is never better pleased than when she sees them under the lash, especially when she suspects her husband of showing to his mulatto children favors which he withholds from his black slaves. The master is frequently compelled to sell this class of his slaves, out of deference to the feelings of his white wife; and, cruel as the deed may strike any one to be, for a man to sell his own children to human flesh-mongers, it is often the dictate of humanity for him to do so; for, unless he does this, he must not only whip them himself, but must stand by and see one white son tie up his brother, of but few shades darker complexion than himself, and ply the gory lash to his naked back; and if he lisp one word of disapproval, it is set down to his parental partiality, and only makes a bad matter worse, both for himself and the slave whom he would protect and defend.

Every year brings with it multitudes of this class of slaves. It was doubtless in consequence of a knowledge of this fact, that one great statesman of the south predicted the downfall of slavery by the inevitable laws of population. Whether this prophecy is ever fulfilled or not, it is nevertheless plain that a very different-looking class of people are springing up at the south, and are now held in slavery, from those originally brought to this country from Africa; and if their increase will do no other good, it will do away the force of the argument, that God cursed Ham,* and therefore American slavery is right. If the lineal descendants of Ham are alone to be scripturally enslaved, it is certain that slavery at the south must soon become unscriptural; for thousands are ushered into the world, annually, who, like myself, owe their existence to white fathers, and those fathers most frequently their own masters.

I have had two masters. My first master's name was Anthony. I do not remember his first name. He was generally called Captain

Anthony—a title which, I presume, he acquired by sailing a craft on the Chesapeake Bay. He was not considered a rich slaveholder. He owned two or three farms, and about thirty slaves. His farms and slaves were under the care of an overseer. The overseer's name was Plummer. Mr. Plummer was a miserable drunkard, a profane swearer, and a savage monster. He always went armed with a cowskin* and a heavy cudgel. I have known him to cut and slash the women's heads so horribly, that even master would be enraged at his cruelty, and would threaten to whip him if he did not mind himself. Master, however, was not a humane slaveholder. It required extraordinary barbarity on the part of an overseer to affect him. He was a cruel man, hardened by a long life of slaveholding. He would at times seem to take great pleasure in whipping a slave. I have often been awakened at the dawn of day by the most heart-rending shrieks of an own aunt of mine, whom he used to tie up to a joist, and whip upon her naked back till she was literally covered with blood. No words, no tears, no prayers, from his gory victim, seemed to move his iron heart from its bloody purpose. The louder she screamed, the harder he whipped; and where the blood ran fastest, there he whipped longest. He would whip her to make her scream, and whip her to make her hush; and not until overcome by fatigue, would he cease to swing the blood-clotted cowskin. I remember the first time I ever witnessed this horrible exhibition. I was quite a child, but I well remember it. I never shall forget it whilst I remember any thing. It was the first of a long series of such outrages, of which I was doomed to be a witness and a participant. It struck me with awful force. It was the blood-stained gate, the entrance to the hell of slavery, through which I was about to pass. It was a most terrible spectacle. I wish I could commit to paper the feelings with which I beheld it.

This occurrence took place very soon after I went to live with my old master, and under the following circumstances. Aunt Hester went out one night,—where or for what I do not know,—and happened to be absent when my master desired her presence. He had ordered her not to go out evenings, and warned her that she must never let him catch her in company with a young man, who was paying attention to her, belonging to Colonel Lloyd. The young man's name was Ned Roberts, generally called Lloyd's Ned. Why master was so careful of her, may be safely left to conjecture. She was a woman of noble form, and of graceful proportions, having very few equals, and fewer superiors, in personal appearance, among the colored or white women of our neighborhood.

Aunt Hester had not only disobeyed his orders in going out, but had been found in company with Lloyd's Ned; which circumstance, I found, from what he said while whipping her, was the chief offence. Had he been a man of pure morals himself, he might have been thought interested in protecting the innocence of my aunt; but those who knew him will not suspect him of any such virtue. Before he commenced whipping Aunt Hester, he took her into the kitchen, and stripped her from neck to waist, leaving her neck, shoulders, and back, entirely naked. He then told her to cross her hands, calling her at the same time a d—d b—h. After crossing her hands, he tied them with a strong rope, and led her to a stool under a large hook in the joist, put in for the purpose. He made her get upon the stool, and tied her hands to the hook. She now stood fair for his infernal purpose. Her arms were stretched up at their full length, so that she stood upon the ends of her toes. He then said to her, "Now, you d—d b—h I'll learn you how to disobey my orders!" and after rolling up his sleeves, he commenced to lay on the heavy cowskin, and soon the warm, red blood (amid heart-rending shrieks from her, and horrid oaths from him) came dripping to the floor. I was so terrified and horror-stricken at the sight, that I hid myself in a closet, and dared not venture out till long after the bloody transaction was over. I expected it would be my turn next. It was all new to me. I had never seen any thing like it before. I had always lived with my grandmother on the outskirts of the plantation, where she was put to raise the children of the younger women. I had therefore been, until now, out of the way of the bloody scenes that often occurred on the plantation.

CHAPTER II

My master's family consisted of two sons, Andrew and Richard; one daughter, Lucretia, and her husband, Captain Thomas Auld. They lived in one house, upon the home plantation of Colonel Edward Lloyd. My master was Colonel Lloyd's clerk and superintendent. He was what might be called the overseer of the overseers. I spent two years of childhood on this plantation in my old master's family. It was here that I witnessed the bloody transaction recorded in the first chapter; and as I received my first impressions of slavery on this plantation, I will give some description of it, and of slavery as it there existed. The plantation is about twelve miles north of Easton, in Talbot county, and is situated on the border of Miles River. The principal products raised upon it were tobacco, corn, and wheat. These were raised in great abundance; so that, with the products of this and the other farms belonging to him, he was able to keep in almost constant employment a large sloop, in carrying them to market at Baltimore. This sloop was named Sally Lloyd, in honor of one of the colonel's daughters. My master's son-in-law, Captain Auld, was master of the vessel; she was otherwise manned by the colonel's own slaves. Their names were Peter, Isaac, Rich, and Jake. These were esteemed very highly by the other slaves, and looked upon as the privileged ones of the plantation; for it was no small affair, in the eyes of the slaves, to be allowed to see Baltimore.

Colonel Lloyd kept from three to four hundred slaves on his home plantation, and owned a large number more on the neighboring farms belonging to him. The names of the farms nearest to the home plantation were Wye Town and New Design. "Wye Town" was under the overseership of a man named Noah Willis. New Design was under the overseership of a Mr. Townsend. The overseers of these, and all the rest of the farms, numbering over twenty, received advice and direction from the managers of the home plantation. This was the great business place. It was the seat of government for the whole twenty farms. All disputes among the overseers were settled here. If a slave was convicted of any high misdemeanor, became unmanageable, or evinced a determination to run away, he was brought immediately here, severely whipped, put on board the sloop, carried to Baltimore, and sold to Austin Woolfolk or some other slave-trader, as a warning to the slaves remaining.

Here, too, the slaves of all the other farms received their monthly allowance of food, and their yearly clothing. The men and women slaves received, as their monthly allowance of food, eight pounds of pork, or its equivalent in fish, and one bushel of corn meal. Their yearly clothing consisted of two coarse linen shirts, one pair of linen trousers, like the shirts, one jacket, one pair of trousers for winter, made of coarse negro cloth, one pair of stockings, and one pair of shoes; the whole of which could not have cost more than seven dollars. The allowance of the slave children was given to their mothers, or the old women having the care of them. The children unable to work in the field had neither shoes, stockings, jackets, nor trousers, given to them; their clothing consisted of two coarse linen shirts per year. When these failed them, they went naked until the next allowance-day. Children from seven to ten years old, of both sexes, almost naked, might be seen at all seasons of the year.

There were no beds given the slaves, unless one coarse blanket be considered such, and none but the men and women had these. This, however, is not considered a very great privation. They find less difficulty from the want of beds, than from the want of time to sleep; for when their day's work in the field is done, the most of them having their washing, mending, and cooking to do, and having few or none of the ordinary facilities for doing either of these, very many of their sleeping hours are consumed in preparing for the field the coming day; and when this is done, old and young, male and female, married and single, drop down side by side, on one common bed,—the cold, damp floor,—each covering himself or herself with their miserable blankets; and here they sleep till they are summoned to the field by the driver's horn. At the sound of this, all must rise, and be off to the field. There must be no halting; every one must be at his or her post; and woe betides them who hear not this morning summons to the field; for if they are not awakened by the sense of hearing, they are by the sense of feeling; no age nor sex finds any favor. Mr. Severe, the overseer, used to stand by the door of the quarter, armed with a large hickory stick and heavy cowskin, ready to whip any one who was so unfortunate as not to hear, or, from any other cause, was prevented from being ready to start for the field at the sound of the horn.

Mr. Severe was rightly named: he was a cruel man. I have seen him whip a woman, causing the blood to run half an hour at the time; and this, too, in the midst of her crying children, pleading for their mother's release. He seemed to take pleasure in manifesting his fiendish barbarity. Added to his cruelty, he was a profane swearer. It was enough to chill the blood and stiffen the hair of an ordinary man to hear him talk. Scarce a sentence escaped him but that was commenced or concluded by some horrid oath. The field was the place to witness his cruelty and profanity. His presence made it both the field of blood and of blasphemy. From the rising till the going down of the sun, he was cursing, raving, cutting, and slashing among the slaves of the field, in the most frightful manner. His career was short. He died very soon after I went to Colonel Lloyd's; and he died as he lived, uttering, with his dying groans, bitter curses and horrid oaths. His death was regarded by the slaves as the result of a merciful providence.

Mr. Severe's place was filled by a Mr. Hopkins. He was a very different man. He was less cruel, less profane, and made less noise, than Mr. Severe. His course was characterized by no extraordinary demonstrations of cruelty. He whipped, but seemed to take no pleasure in it. He was called by the slaves a good overseer.

The home plantation of Colonel Lloyd wore the appearance of a country village. All the mechanical operations for all the farms were performed here. The shoemaking and mending, the blacksmithing, cartwrighting, coopering, weaving, and grain-grinding, were all performed by the slaves on the home plantation. The whole place wore a business-like aspect very unlike the neighboring farms. The number of houses, too, conspired to give it advantage over the neighboring farms. It was called by the slaves the *Great House Farm*. Few privileges were esteemed higher, by the slaves of the out-farms, than that of being selected to do errands at the Great House Farm. It was associated in their minds with greatness. A representative could not be prouder of his election to a seat in the American Congress, than a slave on one of the out-farms would be of his election to do errands at the Great House Farm. They regarded it as evidence of great confidence reposed in them by their overseers; and it was on this account, as well as a constant desire to be out of the field from under the driver's lash, that they esteemed it a high privilege, one worth careful living for. He was called the smartest and most trusty fellow, who had this honor conferred upon him the most frequently. The competitors for this office sought as diligently to please their overseers, as the office-seekers in the political parties seek to please and deceive the people. The same traits of character might be seen in Colonel Lloyd's slaves, as are seen in the slaves of the political parties.

The slaves selected to go to the Great House Farm, for the monthly allowance for themselves and their fellow-slaves, were peculiarly enthusiastic. While on their way, they would make the dense old woods, for miles around, reverberate with their wild songs, revealing at once the highest joy and the deepest sadness. They would compose and sing as they went along, consulting neither time nor tune. The thought that came up, came out—if not in the word, in the sound;—and as frequently in the one as in the other. They would sometimes sing the most pathetic sentiment in the most rapturous tone, and the most rapturous sentiment in the most pathetic tone. Into all of their songs they would manage to weave something of the Great House Farm. Especially would they do this, when leaving home. They would then sing most exultingly the following words:—

> "I am going away to the Great House Farm!
> O, yea! O, yea! O!"

This they would sing, as a chorus, to words which to many would seem unmeaning jargon, but which, nevertheless, were full of

meaning to themselves. I have sometimes thought that the mere
hearing of those songs would do more to impress some minds
with the horrible character of slavery, than the reading of whole
volumes of philosophy on the subject could do.

I did not, when a slave, understand the deep meaning of those
rude and apparently incoherent songs. I was myself within the
circle; so that I neither saw nor heard as those without might see
and hear. They told a tale of woe which was then altogether
beyond my feeble comprehension; they were tones loud, long,
and deep; they breathed the prayer and complaint of souls boiling
over with the bitterest anguish. Every tone was a testimony
against slavery, and a prayer to God for deliverance from chains.
The hearing of those wild notes always depressed my spirit, and
filled me with ineffable sadness. I have frequently found myself
in tears while hearing them. The mere recurrence to those
songs, even now, afflicts me; and while I am writing these lines,
an expression of feeling has already found its way down my
cheek. To those songs I trace my first glimmering conception of
the dehumanizing character of slavery. I can never get rid of
that conception. Those songs still follow me, to deepen my
hatred of slavery, and quicken my sympathies for my brethren
in bonds. If any one wishes to be impressed with the soul-
killing effects of slavery, let him go to Colonel Lloyd's plantation, and, on allowance-day, place himself in the deep pine
woods, and there let him, in silence, analyze the sounds that
shall pass through the chambers of his soul,—and if he is not
thus impressed, it will only be because "there is no flesh in his
obdurate heart."*

I have often been utterly astonished, since I came to the north,
to find persons who could speak of the singing, among slaves, as
evidence of their contentment and happiness. It is impossible to
conceive of a greater mistake. Slaves sing most when they are
most unhappy. The songs of the slave represent the sorrows of his
heart; and he is relieved by them, only as an aching heart is
relieved by its tears. At least, such is my experience. I have often
sung to drown my sorrow, but seldom to express my happiness.
Crying for joy, and singing for joy, were alike uncommon to

me while in the jaws of slavery. The singing of a man cast away upon a desolate island might be as appropriately considered as evidence of contentment and happiness, as the singing of a slave; the songs of the one and of the other are prompted by the same emotion.

CHAPTER III

Colonel Lloyd kept a large and finely cultivated garden, which afforded almost constant employment for four men, besides the chief gardener, (Mr. M'Durmond.) This garden was probably the greatest attraction of the place. During the summer months, people came from far and near—from Baltimore, Easton, and Annapolis—to see it. It abounded in fruits of almost every description, from the hardy apple of the north to the delicate orange of the south. This garden was not the least source of trouble on the plantation. Its excellent fruit was quite a temptation to the hungry swarms of boys, as well as the older slaves, belonging to the colonel, few of whom had the virtue or the vice to resist it. Scarcely a day passed, during the summer, but that some slave had to take the lash for stealing fruit. The colonel had to resort to all kinds of stratagems to keep his slaves out of the garden. The last and most successful one was that of tarring his fence all around; after which, if a slave was caught with any tar upon his person, it was deemed sufficient proof that he had either been into the garden, or had tried to get in. In either case, he was severely whipped by the chief gardener. This plan worked well; the slaves became as fearful of tar as of the lash. They seemed to realize the impossibility of touching *tar* without being defiled.*

The colonel also kept a splendid riding equipage. His stable and carriage-house presented the appearance of some of our large city livery establishments. His horses were of the finest form and noblest blood. His carriage-house contained three splendid coaches, three or four gigs, besides dearborns and barouches* of the most fashionable style.

This establishment was under the care of two slaves—old Barney and young Barney—father and son. To attend to this establishment was their sole work. But it was by no means an easy employment; for in nothing was Colonel Lloyd more particular than in the management of his horses. The slightest inattention to these was unpardonable, and was visited upon those, under whose care they were placed, with the severest punishment; no excuse could shield them, if the colonel only suspected any want of attention to his horses—a supposition which he frequently indulged, and one which, of course, made the office of old and young Barney a very trying one. They never knew when they were safe from punishment. They were frequently whipped when least deserving, and escaped whipping when most deserving it. Every thing depended upon the looks of the horses, and the state of Colonel Lloyd's own mind when his horses were brought to him for use. If a horse did not move fast enough, or hold his head high enough, it was owing to some fault of his keepers. It was painful to stand near the stable-door, and hear the various complaints against the keepers when a horse was taken out for use. "This horse has not had proper attention. He has not been sufficiently rubbed and curried, or he has not been properly fed; his food was too wet or too dry; he got it too soon or too late; he was too hot or too cold; he had too much hay, and not enough of grain; or he had too much grain, and not enough of hay; instead of old Barney's attending to the horse, he had very improperly left it to his son." To all these complaints, no matter how unjust, the slave must answer never a word. Colonel Lloyd could not brook any contradiction from a slave. When he spoke, a slave must stand, listen, and tremble; and such was literally the case. I have seen Colonel Lloyd make old Barney, a man between fifty and sixty years of age, uncover his bald head, kneel down upon the cold, damp ground, and receive upon his naked and toil-worn shoulders more than thirty lashes at the time. Colonel Lloyd had three sons—Edward, Murray, and Daniel,—and three sons-in-law, Mr. Winder, Mr. Nicholson, and Mr. Lowndes. All of these lived at the Great House Farm, and enjoyed the luxury of whipping the servants when they pleased, from old Barney down to William Wilkes, the coach-driver. I have seen Winder make one of the house-servants stand off from him a suitable distance to be touched with the end of his whip, and at every stroke raise great ridges upon his back.

To describe the wealth of Colonel Lloyd would be almost equal to describing the riches of Job.* He kept from ten to fifteen house-servants. He was said to own a thousand slaves, and I think this estimate quite within the truth. Colonel Lloyd owned so many that he did not know them when he saw them; nor did all the slaves of the out-farms know him. It is reported of him, that, while riding along the road one day, he met a colored man, and addressed him in the usual manner of speaking to colored people on the public highways of the south: "Well, boy, whom do you belong to?" "To Colonel Lloyd," replied the slave. "Well, does the colonel treat you well?" "No, sir," was the ready reply. "What, does he work you too hard?" "Yes, sir." "Well, don't he give you enough to eat?" "Yes, sir, he gives me enough, such as it is."

The colonel, after ascertaining where the slave belonged, rode on; the man also went on about his business, not dreaming that he had been conversing with his master. He thought, said, and heard nothing more of the matter, until two or three weeks afterwards. The poor man was then informed by his overseer that, for having found fault with his master, he was now to be sold to a Georgia trader. He was immediately chained and handcuffed; and thus, without a moment's warning, he was snatched away, and forever sundered, from his family and friends, by a hand more unrelenting than death. This is the penalty of telling the truth, of telling the simple truth, in answer to a series of plain questions.

It is partly in consequence of such facts, that slaves when inquired of as to their condition and the character of their masters, almost universally say they are contented, and that their masters are kind. The slaveholders have been known to send in spies among their slaves, to ascertain their views and feelings in regard to their condition. The frequency of this has had the effect to establish among the slaves the maxim, that a still tongue makes a wise head. They suppress the truth rather than take the consequences of telling it, and in so doing prove themselves a part of the human family. If they have any thing to say of their masters, it is generally in their masters' favor, especially when speaking to an untried man. I have been frequently asked, when a slave, if I had a kind master, and do not remember ever to have given a negative answer; nor did I, in pursuing this course, consider myself as uttering what was absolutely false; for I always measured the kindness of my master by the standard of kindness set up among slaveholders around us. Moreover, slaves are like other people, and imbibe prejudices quite common to others. They think their own better than that of others. Many, under the influence of this prejudice, think their own masters are better than the masters of other slaves; and this, too, in some cases, when the very reverse is true. Indeed, it is not uncommon for slaves even to fall out and quarrel among themselves about the relative goodness of their masters, each contending for the superior goodness of his own over that of the others. At the very same time, they mutually execrate their masters when viewed separately. It was so on our plantation. When Colonel Lloyd's slaves met the slaves of Jacob Jepson, they seldom parted without a quarrel about their masters; Colonel Lloyd's slaves contending that he was the richest, and Mr. Jepson's slaves that he was the smartest, and most of a man. Colonel Lloyd's slaves would boast his ability to buy and sell Jacob Jepson. Mr. Jepson's slaves would boast his ability to whip Colonel Lloyd. These quarrels would almost always end in a fight between the parties, and those that whipped were supposed to have gained the point at issue. They seemed to think that the greatness of their masters was transferable to themselves. It was considered as being bad enough to be a slave; but to be a poor man's slave was deemed a disgrace indeed!

CHAPTER IV

Mr. Hopkins remained but a short time in the office of overseer. Why his career was so short, I do not know, but suppose he lacked the necessary severity to suit Colonel Lloyd. Mr. Hopkins was succeeded by Mr. Austin Gore, a man possessing, in an eminent degree, all those traits of character indispensable to what is called a first-rate overseer. Mr. Gore had served Colonel Lloyd, in the capacity of overseer, upon one of the out-farms, and had shown himself worthy of the high station of overseer upon the home or Great House Farm.

Mr. Gore was proud, ambitious, and persevering. He was artful, cruel, and obdurate. He was just the man for such a place, and it was just the place for such a man. It afforded scope for the full exercise of all his powers, and he seemed to be perfectly at home in it. He was one of those who could torture the slightest look, word, or gesture, on the part of the slave, into impudence, and would treat it accordingly. There must be no answering back to him; no explanation was allowed a slave, showing himself to have been wrongfully accused. Mr. Gore acted fully up to the maxim laid down by slaveholders,—"It is better that a dozen slaves suffer under the lash, than that the overseer should be convicted, in the presence of the slaves, of having been at fault." No matter how innocent a slave might be—it availed him nothing, when accused by Mr. Gore of any misdemeanor. To be accused was to be convicted, and to be convicted was to be punished; the one always following the other with immutable certainty. To escape punishment was to escape accusation; and few slaves had the fortune to do either, under the overseership of Mr. Gore. He was just proud enough to demand the most debasing homage of the slave, and quite servile enough to crouch, himself, at the feet of the master. He was ambitious enough to be contented with nothing short of the highest rank of overseers, and persevering enough to reach the height of his ambition. He was cruel enough to inflict the severest punishment, artful enough to descend to the lowest trickery, and obdurate enough to be insensible to the voice of a reproving conscience. He was, of all the overseers, the most dreaded by the slaves. His presence was painful; his eye flashed confusion; and seldom was his sharp, shrill voice heard, without producing horror and trembling in their ranks.

Mr. Gore was a grave man, and, though a young man, he indulged in no jokes, said no funny words, seldom smiled. His words were in perfect keeping with his looks, and his looks were in perfect keeping with his words. Overseers will sometimes indulge in a witty word, even with the slaves; not so with Mr. Gore. He spoke but to command, and commanded but to be obeyed; he dealt sparingly with his words, and bountifully with his whip, never using the former where the latter would answer as well. When he whipped, he seemed to do so from a sense of duty, and feared no consequences. He did nothing reluctantly, no matter how disagreeable; always at his post, never inconsistent. He never promised but to fulfil. He was, in a word, a man of the most inflexible firmness and stone-like coolness.

His savage barbarity was equalled only by the consummate coolness with which he committed the grossest and most savage deeds upon the slaves under his charge. Mr. Gore once undertook to whip one of Colonel Lloyd's slaves, by the name of Demby. He had given Demby but few stripes, when, to get rid of the scourging, he ran and plunged himself into a creek, and stood there at the depth of his shoulders, refusing to come out. Mr. Gore told him that he would give him three calls, and that, if he did not come out at the third call, he would shoot him. The first call was given. Demby made no response, but stood his ground. The second and third calls were given with the same result. Mr. Gore then, without consultation or deliberation with any one, not even giving Demby an additional call, raised his musket to his face, taking deadly aim at his standing victim, and in an instant poor Demby was no more. His mangled body sank out of sight, and blood and brains marked the water where he had stood.

A thrill of horror flashed through every soul upon the plantation, excepting Mr. Gore. He alone seemed cool and collected. He was asked by Colonel Lloyd and my old master, why he resorted to this extraordinary expedient. His reply was, (as well as I can remember,) that Demby had become unmanageable. He was setting a dangerous example to the other slaves,—one which, if suffered to pass without some such demonstration on his part, would finally lead to the total subversion of all rule and order upon the plantation. He argued that if one slave refused to be corrected, and escaped with his life, the other slaves would soon copy the example; the result of which would be, the freedom of the slaves, and the enslavement of the whites. Mr. Gore's defence was satisfactory. He was continued in his station as overseer upon the home plantation. His fame as an overseer went abroad. His horrid crime was not even submitted to judicial investigation. It was committed in the presence of slaves, and they of course could neither institute a suit, nor testify against him; and thus the guilty perpetrator of one of the bloodiest and most foul murders goes unwhipped of justice, and uncensured by the community in which he lives. Mr. Gore lived in St. Michael's, Talbot country, Maryland, when I left there; and if he is still alive, he very probably lives there now; and if so, he is now, as he was then, as highly esteemed and as much respected as though his guilty soul had not been stained with his brother's blood.

I speak advisedly when I say this,—that killing a slave, or any colored person, in Talbot country, Maryland, is not treated as a crime, either by the courts or the community. Mr. Thomas Lanman, of St. Michael's, killed two slaves, one of whom he killed with a hatchet, by knocking his brains out. He used to boast of the commission of the awful and bloody deed. I have heard him do so laughingly, saying, among other things, that he was the only benefactor of his country in the company, and that when others would do as much as he had done, we should be relieved of "the d—d niggers."

The wife of Mr. Giles Hick, living but a short distance from where I used to live, murdered my wife's cousin, a young girl between fifteen and sixteen years of age, mangling her person in the most horrible manner, breaking her nose and breastbone with a stick, so that the poor girl expired in a few hours afterward. She was immediately buried, but had not been in her untimely grave but a few hours before she was taken up and examined by the coroner, who decided that she had come to her death by severe beating. The offence for which this girl was thus murdered was this:—She had been set that night to mind Mrs. Hick's baby, and during the night she fell asleep, and the baby cried. She, having lost her rest for several nights previous, did not hear the crying. They were both in the room with Mrs. Hicks. Mrs. Hicks, finding the girl slow to move, jumped from her bed, seized an oak stick of wood by the fireplace, and with it broke the girl's nose and breastbone, and thus ended her life. I will not say that this most horrid murder produced no sensation in the community. It did produce sensation, but not enough to bring the murderess to punishment. There was a warrant issued for her arrest, but it was never served. Thus she escaped not only punishment, but even the pain of being arraigned before a court for her horrid crime.

Whilst I am detailing bloody deeds which took place during my stay on Colonel Lloyd's plantation, I will briefly narrate another, which occurred about the same time as the murder of Demby by Mr. Gore.

Colonel Lloyd's slaves were in the habit of spending a part of their nights and Sundays in fishing for oysters, and in this way made up the deficiency of their scanty allowance. An old man belonging to Colonel Lloyd, while thus engaged, happened to get beyond the limits of Colonel Lloyd's, and on the premises of Mr. Beal Bondly. At this trespass, Mr. Bondly took offence, and with his musket came down to the shore, and blew its deadly contents into the poor old man.

Mr. Bondly came over to see Colonel Lloyd the next day, whether to pay him for his property, or to justify himself in what he had done, I know not. At any rate, this whole fiendish trans-action was soon hushed up. There was very little said about it at all, and nothing done. It was a common saying, even among little white boys, that it was worth a half-cent to kill a "nigger," and a half-cent to bury one.

CHAPTER V

As to my own treatment while I lived on Colonel Lloyd's planta-tion, it was very similar to that of the other slave children. I was not old enough to work in the field, and there being little else than field work to do, I had a great deal of leisure time. The most I had to do was to drive up the cows at evening, keep the fowls out of the garden, keep the front yard clean, and run of errands for my old master's daughter, Mrs. Lucretia Auld. The most of my leis-ure time I spent in helping Master Daniel Lloyd in finding his birds, after he had shot them. My connection with Master Daniel was of some advantage to me. He became quite attached to me, and was a sort of protector of me. He would not allow the older boys to impose upon me, and would divide his cakes with me.

I was seldom whipped by my old master, and suffered little from any thing else than hunger and cold. In hottest summer and coldest winter, I was kept almost naked—no shoes, no stockings, no jacket, no trousers, nothing on but a coarse tow linen shirt, reaching only to my knees. I had no bed. I must have perished with cold, but that, the coldest nights, I used to steal a bag which was used for carrying corn to the mill. I would crawl into this bag, and there sleep on the cold, damp, clay floor, with my head in and feet out. My feet have been so cracked with the frost, that the pen with which I am writing might be laid in the gashes.

We were not regularly allowanced. Our food was coarse corn meal boiled. This was called *mush*. It was put into a large wooden tray or trough, and set down upon the ground. The children were then called, like so many pigs, and like so many pigs they would come and devour the mush; some with oyster-shells, others with pieces of shingle, some with naked hands, and none with spoons. He that ate fastest got most; he that was strongest secured the best place; and few left the trough satisfied.

I was probably between seven and eight years old when I left Colonel Lloyd's plantation. I left it with joy. I shall never forget the ecstasy with which I received the intelligence that my old master (Anthony) had determined to let me go to Baltimore, to live with Mr. Hugh Auld, brother to my old master's son-in-law, Captain Thomas Auld. I received this information about three days before my departure. They were three of the happiest days I ever enjoyed. I spent the most part of all these three days in the creek, washing off the plantation scurf, and preparing myself for my departure.

The pride of appearance which this would indicate was not my own. I spent the time in washing, not so much because I wished to, but because Mrs. Lucretia had told me I must get all the dead skin off my feet and knees before I could go to Baltimore; for the people in Baltimore were very cleanly, and would laugh at me if I looked dirty. Besides, she was going to give me a pair of trousers, which I should not put on unless I got all the dirt off me. The thought of owning a pair of trousers was great indeed! It was almost a sufficient motive, not only to make me take off what would be called by pig-drovers the mange, but the skin itself. I went at it in good earnest, working for the first time with the hope of reward.

The ties that ordinarily bind children to their homes were all suspended in my case. I found no severe trial in my departure. My home was charmless; it was not home to me; on parting from it, I could not feel that I was leaving any thing which I could have enjoyed by staying. My mother was dead, my grandmother lived far off, so that I seldom saw her. I had two sisters and one brother, that lived in the same house with me; but the early separation of us from our mother had well nigh blotted the fact of our relationship from our memories. I looked for home elsewhere, and was confident of finding none which I should relish less than the one which I was leaving. If, however, I found in my new home hardship, hunger, whipping, and nakedness, I had the consolation that I should not have escaped any one of them by staying. Having already had more than a taste of them in the house of my old master, and having endured them there, I very naturally inferred my ability to endure them elsewhere, and especially at Baltimore; for I had something of the feeling about Baltimore that is expressed in the proverb, that "being hanged in England is preferable to dying a natural death in Ireland." I had the strongest desire to see Baltimore. Cousin Tom, though not fluent in speech, had inspired me with that desire by his eloquent description of the place. I could never point out any thing at the Great House, no matter how beautiful or powerful, but that he had seen something at Baltimore far exceeding, both in beauty and strength, the object which I pointed out to him. Even the Great House itself, with all its pictures, was far inferior to many buildings in Baltimore. So strong was my desire, that I thought a gratification of it would fully compensate for whatever loss of comforts I should sustain by the exchange. I left without a regret, and with the highest hopes of future happiness.

We sailed out of Miles River for Baltimore on a Saturday morning. I remember only the day of the week, for at that time I had no knowledge of the days of the month, nor the months of the year. On setting sail, I walked aft, and gave to Colonel Lloyd's plantation what I hoped would be the last look. I then placed myself in the bows of the sloop, and there spent the remainder of the day in looking ahead, interesting myself in what was in the distance rather than in things near by or behind.

In the afternoon of that day, we reached Annapolis, the capital of the State. We stopped but a few moments, so that I had no time to go on shore. It was the first large town that I had ever seen, and though it would look small compared with some of our New England factory villages, I thought it a wonderful place for its size—more imposing even than the Great House Farm!

We arrived at Baltimore early on Sunday morning, landing at Smith's Wharf, not far from Bowley's Wharf. We had on board the sloop a large flock of sheep; and after aiding in driving them to the slaughter-house of Mr. Curtis on Louden Slater's Hill, I was conducted by Rich, one of the hands belonging on board of the sloop, to my new home in Alliciana Street, near Mr. Gardner's ship-yard, on Fells Point.

Mr. and Mrs. Auld were both at home, and met me at the door with their little son Thomas, to take care of whom I had been given. And here I saw what I had never seen before; it was a white face beaming with the most kindly emotions; it was the face of my new mistress, Sophia Auld. I wish I could describe the rapture that flashed through my soul as I beheld it. It was a new and strange sight to me, brightening up my pathway with the light of happiness. Little Thomas was told, there was his Freddy,—and I was told to take care of little Thomas; and thus I entered upon the duties of my new home with the most cheering prospect ahead.

I look upon my departure from Colonel Lloyd's plantation as one of the most interesting events of my life. It is possible, and even quite probable, that but for the mere circumstance of being removed from that plantation to Baltimore, I should have to-day, instead of being here seated by my own table, in the enjoyment of freedom and the happiness of home, writing this Narrative, been confined in the galling chains of slavery. Going to live at Baltimore laid the foundation, and opened the gateway, to all my subsequent prosperity. I have ever regarded it as the first plain manifestation of that kind providence which has ever since attended me, and marked my life with so many favors. I regarded the selection of myself as being somewhat remarkable. There were a number of slave children that might have been sent from the plantation to Baltimore. There were those younger, those older, and those of the same age. I was chosen from among them all, and was the first, last, and only choice.

I may be deemed superstitious, and even egotistical, in regarding this event as a special interposition of divine Providence in my favor. But I should be false to the earliest sentiments of my soul, if I suppressed the opinion. I prefer to be true to myself, even at the hazard of incurring the ridicule of others, rather than to be false, and incur my own abhorrence. From my earliest recollection, I date the entertainment of a deep conviction that slavery would not always be able to hold me within its foul embrace; and in the darkest hours of my career in slavery, this living word of faith and spirit of hope departed not from me, but remained like ministering angels to cheer me through the gloom. This good spirit was from God, and to him I offer thanksgiving and praise.

CHAPTER VI

My new mistress proved to be all she appeared when I first met her at the door,—a woman of the kindest heart and finest feelings. She had never had a slave under her control previously to myself, and prior to her marriage she had been dependent upon her own industry for a living. She was by trade a weaver; and by constant application to her business, she had been in a good degree preserved from the blighting and dehumanizing effects of slavery. I was utterly astonished at her goodness. I scarcely knew how to behave towards her. She was entirely unlike any other white woman I had ever seen. I could not approach her as I was accustomed to approach other white ladies. My early instruction was all out of place. The crouching servility, usually so acceptable a quality in a slave, did not answer when manifested toward her. Her favor was not gained by it; she seemed to be disturbed by it. She did not deem it impudent or unmannerly for a slave to look her in the face. The meanest slave was put fully at ease in her presence, and none left without feeling better for having seen her. Her face was made of heavenly smiles, and her voice of tranquil music.

But, alas! this kind heart had but a short time to remain such. The fatal poison of irresponsible power was already in her hands, and soon commenced its infernal work. That cheerful eye, under the influence of slavery, soon became red with rage; that voice, made all of sweet accord, changed to one of harsh and horrid discord; and that angelic face gave place to that of a demon.

Very soon after I went to live with Mr. and Mrs. Auld, she very kindly commenced to teach me the A, B, C. After I had learned this, she assisted me in learning to spell words of three or four letters. Just at this point of my progress, Mr. Auld found out what was going on, and at once forbade Mrs. Auld to instruct me further, telling her, among other things, that it was unlawful, as well as unsafe, to teach a slave to read. To use his own words, further, he said, "If you give a nigger an inch, he will take an ell. A nigger should know nothing but to obey his master—to do as he is told to do. Learning would *spoil* the best nigger in the world. Now," said he, "if you teach that nigger (speaking of myself) how to read, there would be no keeping him. It would forever unfit him to be a slave. He would at once become unmanageable, and of no value to his master. As to himself, it could do him no good, but a great deal of harm. It would make him discontented and unhappy." These words sank deep into my heart, stirred up sentiments within that lay slumbering, and called into existence an entirely new train of thought. It was a new and special revelation, explaining dark and mysterious things, with which my youthful understanding had struggled, but struggled in vain. I now understood what had been to me a most perplexing difficulty—to wit, the white man's power to enslave the black man. It was a grand achievement, and I prized it highly. From that moment, I understood the pathway from slavery to freedom. It was just what I wanted, and I got it at a time when I the least expected it. Whilst I was saddened by the thought of losing the aid of my kind mistress, I was gladdened by the invaluable instruction which, by the merest accident, I had gained from my master. Though conscious of the difficulty of learning without a teacher, I set out with high hope, and a fixed purpose, at whatever cost of trouble, to learn how to read. The very decided manner with which he spoke, and strove to impress his wife with the evil consequences of giving me instruction, served to convince me that he was deeply sensible of the truths he was uttering. It gave me the best assurance that I might rely with the utmost confidence on the results which, he said, would flow from teaching me to read. What he most dreaded, that I most desired. What he most loved, that I most hated. That which to him was a great evil, to be carefully shunned, was to me a great good, to be diligently sought; and the argument which he so warmly urged, against my learning to read, only served to inspire me with a desire and determination to learn. In learning to read, I owe almost as much to the bitter opposition of my master, as to the kindly aid of my mistress. I acknowledge the benefit of both.

I had resided but a short time in Baltimore before I observed a marked difference, in the treatment of slaves, from that which I had witnessed in the country. A city slave is almost a freeman, compared with a slave on the plantation. He is much better fed and clothed, and enjoys privileges altogether unknown to the slave on the plantation. There is a vestige of decency, a sense of shame, that does much to curb and check those outbreaks of atrocious cruelty so commonly enacted upon the plantation. He is a desperate slaveholder, who will shock the humanity of his non-slaveholding neighbors with the cries of his lacerated slave. Few are willing to incur the odium attaching to the reputation of being a cruel master; and above all things, they would not be known as not giving a slave enough to eat. Every city slaveholder is anxious to have it known of him, that he feeds his slaves well; and it is due to them to say, that most of them do give their slaves enough to eat. There are, however, some painful exceptions to this rule. Directly opposite to us, on Philpot Street, lived Mr. Thomas Hamilton. He owned two slaves. Their names were Henrietta and Mary. Henrietta was about twenty-two years of age, Mary was about fourteen; and of all the mangled and emaciated creatures I ever looked upon, these two were the most so. His heart must be harder than stone, that could look upon these unmoved. The head, neck, and shoulders of Mary were literally cut to pieces. I have frequently felt her head, and found it nearly covered with festering sores, caused by the lash of her cruel mistress. I do not know that her master ever whipped her, but I have been an eye-witness to the cruelty of Mrs. Hamilton. I used to be in Mr. Hamilton's house nearly every day. Mrs. Hamilton used to sit in a large chair in the middle of the room, with a heavy cowskin always by her side, and scarce an hour passed during the day but was marked by the blood of one of these slaves. The girls seldom passed her without her saying, "Move faster, you *black gip!*"* at the same time giving them a blow with the cowskin over the head or shoulders, often drawing the blood. She would then say, "Take that, you *black gip!*"—continuing, "If you don't move faster, I'll move you!" Added to the cruel lashings to which these slaves were subjected, they were kept nearly half-starved. They seldom knew what it was to eat a full meal. I have seen Mary contending with the pigs for the offal thrown into the street. So much was Mary kicked and cut to pieces, that she was oftener called *"pecked"* than by her name.

CHAPTER VII

I lived in Master Hugh's family about seven years. During this time, I succeeded in learning to read and write. In accomplishing this, I was compelled to resort to various stratagems. I had no regular teacher. My mistress, who had kindly commenced to instruct me, had, in compliance with the advice and direction of her husband, not only ceased to instruct, but had set her face against my being instructed by any one else. It is due, however, to my mistress to say of her, that she did not adopt this course of treatment immediately. She at first lacked the depravity indispensable to shutting me up in mental darkness. It was at least necessary for her to have some training in the exercise of irresponsible power, to make her equal to the task of treating me as though I were a brute.

My mistress was, as I have said, a kind and tender-hearted woman; and in the simplicity of her soul she commenced, when I first went to live with her, to treat me as she supposed one human being ought to treat another. In entering upon the duties of a slaveholder, she did not seem to perceive that I sustained to her the relation of a mere chattel, and that for her to treat me as a human being was not only wrong, but dangerously so. Slavery proved as injurious to her as it did to me. When I went there, she was a pious, warm, and tender-hearted woman. There was no sorrow or suffering for which she had not a tear. She had bread for the hungry, clothes for the naked, and comfort for every mourner that came within her reach. Slavery soon proved its ability to divest her of these heavenly qualities. Under its influence, the tender heart became stone, and the lamblike disposition gave way to one of tiger-like fierceness. The first step in her downward course was in her ceasing to instruct me. She now commenced to practise her husband's precepts. She finally became even more violent in her opposition than her husband himself. She was not satisfied with simply doing as well as he had commanded; she seemed anxious to do better. Nothing seemed to make her more angry than to see me with a newspaper. She seemed to think that here lay the danger. I have had her rush at me with a face made all up of fury, and snatch from me a newspaper, in a manner that fully revealed her apprehension. She was an apt woman; and a little experience soon demonstrated, to her satisfaction, that education and slavery were incompatible with each other.

From this time I was most narrowly watched. If I was in a separate room any considerable length of time, I was sure to be suspected of having a book, and was at once called to give an account of myself. All this, however, was too late. The first step had been taken. Mistress, in teaching me the alphabet, had given me the *inch*, and no precaution could prevent me from taking the *ell*.

The plan which I adopted, and the one by which I was most successful, was that of making friends of all the little white boys whom I met in the street. As many of these as I could, I converted into teachers. With their kindly aid, obtained at different times and in different places, I finally succeeded in learning to read. When I was sent of errands, I always took my book with me, and by going one part of my errand quickly, I found time to get a lesson before my return. I used also to carry bread with me, enough of which was always in the house, and to which I was always welcome; for I was much better off in this regard than many of the poor white children in our neighborhood. This bread I used to bestow upon the hungry little urchins, who, in return, would give me that more valuable bread of knowledge. I am strongly tempted to give the names of two or three of those little boys, as a testimonial of the gratitude and affection I bear them; but prudence forbids;—not that it would injure me, but it might embarrass them; for it is almost an unpardonable offence to teach slaves to read in this Christian country. It is enough to say of the dear little fellows, that they lived on Philpot Street, very near Durgin and Bailey's shipyard. I used to talk this matter of slavery over with them. I would sometimes say to them, I wished I could be as free as they would be when they got to be men. "You will be free as soon as you are twenty-one, *but I am a slave for life!* Have not I as good a right to be free as you have?" These words used to trouble them; they would express for me the liveliest sympathy, and console me with the hope that something would occur by which I might be free.

I was now about twelve years old, and the thought of being *a slave for life* began to bear heavily upon my heart. Just about this time, I got hold of a book entitled "The Columbian orator."* Every opportunity I got, I used to read this book. Among much of other interesting matter, I found in it a dialogue between a master and his slave. The slave was represented as having run away from his master three times. The dialogue represented the conversation which took place between them, when the slave was retaken the third time. In this dialogue, the whole argument in behalf of slavery was brought forward by the master, all of which was disposed of by the slave. The slave was made to say some very smart as well as impressive things in reply to his master—things which had the desired though unexpected effect; for the conversation resulted in the voluntary emancipation of the slave on the part of the master.

In the same book, I met with one of Sheridan's mighty speeches* on and in behalf of Catholic emancipation.* These were choice documents to me. I read them over and over again with unabated interest. They gave tongue to interesting thoughts of my own soul, which had frequently flashed through my mind, and died away for want of utterance. The moral which I gained from the dialogue was the power of truth over the conscience of even a slaveholder. What I got from Sheridan was a bold denunciation of slavery, and a powerful vindication of human rights. The reading of these documents enabled me to utter my thoughts, and to meet the arguments brought forward to sustain slavery; but while they relieved me of one difficulty, they brought on another even more painful than the one of which I was relieved. The more I read, the more I was led to abhor and detest my enslavers. I could regard them in no other light than a band of successful robbers, who had left their homes, and gone to Africa, and stolen us from our homes, and in a strange land reduced us to slavery. I loathed them as being the meanest as well as the most wicked of men. As I read and contemplated the subject, behold! that very discontentment which Master Hugh had predicted would follow my learning to read had already come, to torment and sting my soul to unutterable anguish. As I writhed under it, I would at times feel that learning to read had been a curse rather than a blessing. It had given me a view of my wretched condition, without the remedy. I opened my eyes to the horrible pit, but to no ladder upon which to get out. In moments of agony, I envied my fellow-slaves for their stupidity. I have often wished myself a beast. I preferred the condition of the meanest reptile to my own. Any thing, no matter what, to get rid of thinking! It was this everlasting thinking of my condition that tormented me. There was no getting rid of it. It was pressed upon me by every object within sight or hearing, animate or inanimate. The silver trump of freedom had roused my soul to eternal wakefulness. Freedom now appeared, to disappear no more forever. It was heard in every sound, and seen in every thing. It was ever present to torment me with a sense of my wretched condition. I saw nothing without seeing it, I heard nothing without hearing it, and felt nothing without feeling it. It looked from every star, it smiled in every calm, breathed in every wind, and moved in every storm.

I often found myself regretting my own existence, and wishing myself dead; and but for the hope of being free, I have no doubt but that I should have killed myself, or done something for which I should have been killed. While in this state of mind, I was eager to hear any one speak of slavery. I was a ready listener. Every little while, I could hear something about the abolitionists. It was some time before I found what the word meant. It was always used in such connections as to make it an interesting word to me. If a slave ran away and succeeded in getting clear, or if a slave killed his master, set fire to a barn, or did any thing very wrong in the mind of a slaveholder, it was spoken of as the fruit of *abolition*. Hearing the word in this connection very often, I set about learning what it meant. The dictionary afforded me little or no help. I found it was "the act of abolishing;" but then I did not know what was to be abolished. Here I was perplexed. I did not dare to ask any one about its meaning, for I was satisfied that it was something they wanted me to know very little about. After a patient waiting, I got one of our city papers, containing an account of the number of petitions from the north, praying for the abolition of slavery in the District of Columbia, and of the slave trade between the States. From this time I understood the words *abolition* and *abolitionist*, and always drew near when that word was spoken, expecting to hear something of importance to myself and fellow-slaves. The light broke in upon me by degrees. I went one day down on the wharf of Mr. Waters; and seeing two Irishmen unloading a scow* of stone, I went, unasked, and helped them. When we had finished, one of them came to me and asked me if I were a slave. I told him I was. He asked, "Are ye a slave for life?" I told him that I was. The good Irishman seemed to be deeply affected by the statement. He said to the other that it was a pity so fine a little fellow as myself should be a slave for life. He said it was a shame to hold me. They both advised me to run away to the north; that I should find friends there, and that I should be free. I pretended not to be interested in what they said, and treated them as if I did not understand them; for I feared they might be treacherous. White men have been known to encourage slaves to escape, and then, to get the reward, catch them and return them to their masters. I was afraid that these seemingly good men might use me so; but I nevertheless remembered their advice, and from that time I resolved to run away. I looked forward to a time at which it would be safe for me to escape. I was too young to think of doing so immediately; besides, I wished to learn how to write, as I might have occasion to write my own pass. I consoled myself with the hope that I should one day find a good chance. Meanwhile, I would learn to write.

The idea as to how I might learn to write was suggested to me by being in Durgin and Bailey's ship-yard, and frequently seeing the ship carpenters, after hewing, and getting a piece of timber ready for use, write on the timber the name of that part of the ship for which it was intended. When a piece of timber was intended for the larboard side, it would be marked thus—"L." When a piece was for the starboard side, it would be marked thus—"S." A piece for the larboard side forward, would be marked thus—"L. F." When a piece was for starboard side forward, it would be marked thus—"S. F." For larboard aft, it would be marked thus—"L. A." For starboard aft, it would be marked thus—"S. A." I soon learned the names of these letters, and for what they were intended when placed upon a piece of timber in the shipyard. I immediately commenced copying them, and in a short time was able to make the four letters named. After that, when I met with any boy who I knew could write, I would tell him I could write as well as he. The next word would be, "I don't believe you. Let me see you try it." I would then make the letters which I had been so fortunate as to learn, and ask him to beat that. In this way I got a good many lessons in writing, which it is quite possible I should never have gotten in any other way. During this time, my copy-book was the board fence, brick wall, and pavement; my pen and ink was a lump of chalk. With these, I learned mainly how to write. I then commenced and continued copying the Italics in Webster's Spelling Book,* until I could make them all without looking at the book. By this time, my little Master Thomas had gone to school, and learned how to write, and had written over a number of copy-books. These had been brought home, and shown to some of our near neighbors, and then laid aside. My mistress used to go to class meeting at the Wilk Street meeting-house every Monday afternoon, and leave me to take care of the house. When left thus, I used to spend the time in writing in the spaces left in Master Thomas's copy-book, copying what he had written. I continued to do this until I could write a hand very similar to that of Master Thomas. Thus, after a long, tedious effort for years, I finally succeeded in learning how to write.

CHAPTER VIII

In a very short time after I went to live at Baltimore, my old master's youngest son Richard died; and in about three years and six months after his death, my old master, Captain Anthony, died, leaving only his son, Andrew, and daughter, Lucretia, to share his estate. He died while on a visit to see his daughter at Hills-borough. Cut off thus unexpectedly, he left no will as to the dis-posal of his property. It was therefore necessary to have a valuation of the property, that it might be equally divided between Mrs. Lucretia and Master Andrew. I was immediately sent for, to be valued with the other property. Here again my feelings rose up in detestation of slavery. I had now a new conception of my degraded condition. Prior to this, I had become, if not insensible to my lot, at least partly so. I left Baltimore with a young heart overborne with sadness, and a soul full of apprehension. I took passage with Captain Rowe, in the schooner Wild Cat, and, after a sail of about twenty-four hours, I found myself near the place of my birth. I had now been absent from it almost, if not quite, five years. I, however, remembered the place very well. I was only about five years old when I left it, to go and live with my old master on Colonel Lloyd's plantation; so that I was now between ten and eleven years old.

We were all ranked together at the valuation. Men and women, old and young, married and single, were ranked with horses, sheep, and swine. There were horses and men, cattle and women, pigs and children, all holding the same rank in the scale of being, and were all subjected to the same narrow examination. Silvery-headed age and sprightly youth, maids and matrons, had to undergo the same indelicate inspection. At this moment, I saw more clearly than ever the brutalizing effects of slavery upon both slave and slaveholder.

After the valuation, then came the division. I have no language to express the high excitement and deep anxiety which were felt among us poor slaves during this time. Our fate for life was now to be decided. We had no more voice in that decision than the brutes among whom we were ranked. A single word from the white men was enough—against all our wishes, prayers, and entreaties—to sunder forever the dearest friends, dearest kindred, and strongest ties known to human beings. In addition to the pain of separation, there was the horrid dread of falling into the hands of Master Andrew. He was known to us all as being a most cruel wretch,—a common drunkard, who had, by his reckless mismanagement and profligate dissipation, already wasted a large portion of his father's property. We all felt that we might as well be sold at once to the Georgia traders, as to pass into his hands; for we knew that that would be our inevitable condition,—a condition held by us all in the utmost horror and dread.

I suffered more anxiety than most of my fellow-slaves. I had known what it was to be kindly treated; they had known nothing of the kind. They had seen little or nothing of the world. They were in very deed men and women of sorrow, and acquainted with grief. Their backs had been made familiar with the bloody lash, so that they had become callous; mine was yet tender; for while at Baltimore I got few whippings, and few slaves could boast of a kinder master and mistress than myself; and the thought of passing out of their hands into those of Master Andrew—a man who, but a few days before, to give me a sample of his bloody disposition, took my little brother by the throat, threw him on the ground, and with the heel of his boot stamped upon his head till the blood gushed from his nose and ears— was well calculated to make me anxious as to my fate. After he had committed this savage outrage upon my brother, he turned to me, and said that was the way he meant to serve me one of these days,—meaning, I suppose, when I came into his possession.

Thanks to a kind Providence, I fell to the portion of Mrs. Lucretia, and was sent immediately back to Baltimore, to live again in the family of Master Hugh. Their joy at my return equalled their sorrow at my departure. It was a glad day to me. I had escaped a [fate] worse than lion's jaws. I was absent from

Baltimore, for the purpose of valuation and division, just about one month, and it seemed to have been six.

Very soon after my return to Baltimore, my mistress, Lucretia, died, leaving her husband and one child, Amanda; and in a very short time after her death, Master Andrew died. Now all the property of my old master, slaves included, was in the hands of strangers,—strangers who had had nothing to do with accumulating it. Not a slave was left free. All remained slaves, from the youngest to the oldest. If any one thing in my experience, more than another, served to deepen my conviction of the infernal character of slavery, and to fill me with unutterable loathing of slaveholders, it was their base ingratitude to my poor old grandmother. She had served my old master faithfully from youth to old age. She had been the source of all his wealth; she had peopled his plantation with slaves; she had become a great grandmother in his service. She had rocked him in infancy, attended him in childhood, served him through life, and at his death wiped from his icy brow the cold death-sweat, and closed his eyes forever. She was nevertheless left a slave—a slave for life—a slave in the hands of strangers; and in their hands she saw her children, her grandchildren, and her great-grandchildren, divided, like so many sheep, without being gratified with the small privilege of a single word, as to their or her own destiny. And, to cap the climax of their base ingratitude and fiendish barbarity, my grandmother, who was now very old, having outlived my old master and all his children, having seen the beginning and end of all of them, and her present owners finding she was of but little value, her frame already racked with the pains of old age, and complete helplessness fast stealing over her once active limbs, they took her to the woods, built her a little hut, put up a little mud-chimney, and then made her welcome to the privilege of supporting herself there in perfect loneliness; thus virtually turning her out to die! If my poor old grandmother now lives, she lives to suffer in utter loneliness; she lives to remember and mourn over the loss of children, the loss of grand-children, and the loss of great-grandchildren. They are, in the language of the slave's poet, Whittier,*—

"Gone, gone, sold and gone
To the rice swamp dank and lone,
Where the slave-whip ceaseless swings,
Where the noisome insect stings,
Where the fever-demon strews
Poison with the falling dews,
Where the sickly sunbeams glare
Through the hot and misty air:—
    Gone, gone, sold and gone
    To the rice swamp dank and lone,
    From Virginia hills and waters—
    Woe is me, my stolen daughters!"

The hearth is desolate. The children, the unconscious children, who once sang and danced in her presence, are gone. She gropes her way, in the darkness of age, for a drink of water. Instead of the voices of her children, she hears by day the moans of the dove, and by night the screams of the hideous owl. All is gloom. The grave is at the door. And now, when weighed down by the pains and aches of old age, when the head inclines to the feet, when the beginning and ending of human existence meet, and helpless infancy and painful old age combine together—at this time, this most needful time, the time for the exercise of that tenderness and affection which children only can exercise towards a declining parent—my poor old grandmother, the devoted mother of twelve children, is left all alone, in yonder little hut, before a few dim embers. She stands—she sits—she staggers—she falls—she groans—she dies—and there are none of her children or grandchildren present, to wipe from her wrinkled brow the cold sweat of death, or to place beneath the sod her fallen remains. Will not a righteous God visit for these things?*

In about two years after the death of Mrs. Lucretia, Master Thomas married his second wife. Her name was Rowena Hamilton. She was the eldest daughter of Mr. William Hamilton. Master now lived in St. Michael's. Not long after his marriage, a misunderstanding took place between himself and Master Hugh; and as a means of punishing his brother, he took me from him to live with himself at St. Michael's. Here I underwent another most painful separation. It, however, was not so severe as the one I dreaded at the division of property; for, during this interval, a great change had taken place in Master Hugh and his once kind and affectionate wife. The influence of brandy upon him, and of slavery upon her, had effected a disastrous change in the characters of both; so that, as far as they were concerned, I thought I had little to lose by the change. But it was not to them that I was attached. It was to those little Baltimore boys that I felt the strongest attachment. I had received many good lessons from them, and was still receiving them, and the thought of leaving them was painful indeed. I was leaving, too, without the hope of ever being allowed to return. Master Thomas had said he would never let me return again. The barrier betwixt himself and brother he considered impassable.

I then had to regret that I did not at least make the attempt to carry out my resolution to run away; for the chances of success are tenfold greater from the city than from the country.

I sailed from Baltimore for St. Michael's in the sloop Amanda, Captain Edward Dodson. On my passage, I paid particular attention to the direction which the steamboats took to go to Philadelphia. I found, instead of going down, on reaching North Point they went up the bay, in a north-easterly direction. I deemed this knowledge of the utmost importance. My determination to run away was again revived. I resolved to wait only so long as the offering of a favorable opportunity. When that came, I was determined to be off.

CHAPTER IX

I have now reached a period of my life when I can give dates. I left Baltimore, and went to live with Master Thomas Auld, at St. Michael's, in March, 1832. It was now more than seven years since I lived with him in the family of my old master, on Colonel Lloyd's plantation. We of course were now almost entire strangers to each other. He was to me a new master, and I to him a new slave. I was ignorant of his temper and disposition; he was equally so of mine. A very short time, however, brought us into full acquaintance with each other. I was made acquainted with his wife not less than with himself. They were well matched, being equally mean and cruel. I was now, for the first time during a space of more than seven years, made to feel the painful gnawings of hunger—a something which I had not experienced before since I left Colonel Lloyd's plantation. It went hard enough with me then, when I could look back to no period at which I had enjoyed a sufficiency. It was tenfold harder after living in Master Hugh's family, where I had always had enough to eat, and of that which was good. I have said Master Thomas was a mean man. He was so. Not to give a slave enough to eat, is regarded as the most aggravated development of meanness even among slaveholders. The rule is, no matter how coarse the food, only let there be enough of it. This is the theory; and in the part of Maryland from which I came, it is the general practice,—though there are many exceptions. Master Thomas gave us enough of neither coarse nor fine food. There were four slaves of us in the kitchen—my sister Eliza, my aunt Priscilla, Henny, and myself; and we were allowed less than a half bushel of corn-meal per week, and very little else, either in the shape of meat or vegetables. It was not enough for us to subsist upon. We were therefore reduced to the wretched necessity of living at the expense of our neighbors. This we did by begging and stealing, whichever came handy in the time of need, the one being considered as legitimate as the other. A great many times have we poor creatures been nearly perishing with hunger, when food in abundance lay mouldermg in the safe and smoke-house,* and our pious mistress was aware of the fact; and yet that mistress and her husband would kneel every morning, and pray that God would bless them in basket and store!

Bad as all slaveholders are, we seldom meet one destitute of every element of character commanding respect. My master was one of this rare sort. I do not know of one single noble act ever performed by him. The leading trait in his character was meanness; and if there were any other element in his nature, it was made subject to this. He was mean; and, like most other mean men, he lacked the ability to conceal his meanness. Captain Auld was not born a slaveholder. He bad been a poor man, master only of a Bay craft. He came into possession of all his slaves by marriage; and of all men, adopted slaveholders are the worse. He was cruel, but cowardly. He commanded without firmness. In the enforcement of his rules, he was at times rigid, and at times lax. At times, he spoke to his slaves with the firmness of Napoleon and the fury of a demon; at other times, he might well be mistaken for an inquirer who had lost his way. He did nothing of himself. He might have passed for a lion, but for his ears. In all things noble which he attempted, his own meanness shone most conspicuous. His airs, words, and actions, were the airs, words, and actions of born slaveholders, and, being assumed, were awkward enough. He was not even a good imitator. He possessed all the disposition to deceive, but wanted the power. Having no resources within himself, he was compelled to be the copyist of many, and being such, he was forever the victim of inconsistency; and of consequence he was an object of contempt, and was held as such even by his slaves. The luxury of having slaves of his own to wait upon him was something new and unprepared for. He was a slaveholder without the ability to hold slaves. He found himself incapable of managing his slaves either by force, fear, or fraud. We seldom called him "master," we generally called him "Captain Auld," and were hardly disposed to title him at all. I doubt not that our conduct had much to do with making him appear awkward, and of consequence fretful. Our want of reverence for him must have perplexed him greatly. He wished to have us call him master, but lacked the firmness necessary to command us to do so. His wife used to insist upon our calling him so, but to no purpose. In August, 1832, my master attended a Methodist camp-meeting* held in the Bay-side, Talbot county, and there experienced religion. I indulged a faint hope that his conversion would lead him to emancipate his slaves, and that, if he did not do this, it would, at any rate, make him more kind and humane. I was disappointed in both these respects. It neither made him to be humane to his slaves, nor to emancipate them. If it had any effect on his character, it made him more cruel and hateful in all his ways; for I believe him to have been a much worse man after his conversion than before. Prior to his conversion, he relied upon his own depravity to shield and sustain him in his savage barbarity; but after his conversion, he found religious sanction and support for his slaveholding cruelty. He made the greatest pretensions to piety. His house was the house of prayer. He prayed morning, noon, and night. He very soon distinguished himself among his brethren, and was soon made a class-leader and exhorter. His activity in revivals was great, and he proved himself an instrument in the hands of the church in converting many souls. His house was the preachers' home. They used to take great pleasure in coming there to put up; for while he starved us, he stuffed them. We have had three or four preachers there at a time. The names of those who used to come most frequently while I lived there, were Mr. Storks, Mr. Ewery, Mr. Humphry, and Mr. Hickey. I have also seen Mr. George Cookman at our house. We slaves loved Mr. Cookman. We believed him to be a good man. We thought him instrumental in getting Mr. Samuel Harrison, a very rich slaveholder, to emancipate his slaves; and by some means got the impression that he was laboring to effect the emancipation of all the slaves. When he was at our house, we were sure to be called in to prayers. When the others were there, we were sometimes called in and sometimes not. Mr. Cookman took more notice of us than either of the other ministers. He could not come among us without betraying his sympathy for us, and, stupid as we were, we had the sagacity to see it.

While I lived with my master in St. Michael's, there was a

white young man, a Mr. Wilson, who proposed to keep a Sabbath school for the instruction of such slaves as might be disposed to learn to read the New Testament. We met but three times, when Mr. West and Mr. Fairbanks, both class-leaders, with many others, came upon us with sticks and other missiles, drove us off, and forbade us to meet again. Thus ended our little Sabbath school in the pious town of St. Michael's.

I have said my master found religious sanction for his cruelty. As an example, I will state one of the many facts going to prove the charge. I have seen him tie up a lame young woman, and whip her with a heavy cowskin upon her naked shoulders, causing the warm red blood to drip; and, in justification of the bloody deed, he would quote this passage of Scripture—"He that knoweth his master's will, and doeth it not, shall be beaten with many stripes."*

Master would keep this lacerated young woman tied up in this horrid situation four or five hours at a time. I have known him to tie her up early in the morning, and whip her before breakfast; leave her, go to his store, return at dinner, and whip her again, cutting her in the places already made raw with his cruel lash. The secret of master's cruelty toward "Henny" is found in the fact of her being almost helpless. When quite a child, she fell into the fire, and burned herself horribly. Her hands were so burnt that she never got the use of them. She could do very little but bear heavy burdens. She was to master a bill of expense; and as he was a mean man, she was a constant offence to him. He seemed desirous of getting the poor girl out of existence. He gave her away once to his sister; but, being a poor gift, she was not disposed to keep her. Finally, my benevolent master, to use his own words, "set her adrift to take care of herself." Here was a recently-converted man, holding on upon the mother, and at the same time turning out her helpless child, to starve and die! Master Thomas was one of the many pious slaveholders who hold slaves for the very charitable purpose of taking care of them.

My master and myself had quite a number of differences. He found me unsuitable to his purpose. My city life, he said, had had a very pernicious effect upon me. It had almost ruined me for every good purpose, and fitted me for every thing which was bad. One of my greatest faults was that of letting his horse run away, and go down to his father-in-law's farm, which was about five miles from St. Michael's. I would then have to go after it. My reason for this kind of carelessness, or carefulness, was, that I could always get something to eat when I went there. Master William Hamilton, my master's father-in-law, always gave his slaves enough to eat. I never left there hungry, no matter how great the need of my speedy return. Master Thomas at length said he would stand it no longer. I had lived with him nine months, during which time he had given me a number of severe whippings, all to no good purpose. He resolved to put me out, as he said, to be broken; and, for this purpose, he let me for one year to a man named Edward Covey. Mr. Covey was a poor man, a farm-renter. He rented the place upon which he lived, as also the hands with which he tilled it. Mr. Covey had acquired a very high reputation for breaking young slaves, and this reputation was of immense value to him. It enabled him to get his farm tilled with much less expense to himself than he could have had it done without such a reputation. Some slaveholders thought it not much loss to allow Mr. Covey to have their slaves one year, for the sake of the training to which they were subjected, without any other compensation. He could hire young help with great ease, in consequence of this reputation. Added to the natural good qualities of Mr. Covey, he was a professor of religion—a pious soul— a member and class-leader in the Methodist church. All of this added weight to his reputation as a "nigger-breaker." I was aware of all the facts, having been made acquainted with them by a young man who had lived there. I nevertheless made the change gladly; for I was sure of getting enough to eat, which is not the smallest consideration to a hungry man.

CHAPTER X

I left Master Thomas's house, and went to live with Mr. Covey, on the 1st of January, 1833. I was now, for the first time in my life, a field hand. In my new employment, I found myself even more awkward than a country boy appeared to be in a large city. I had been at my new home but one week before Mr. Covey gave me a very severe whipping, cutting my back, causing the blood to run, and raising ridges on my flesh as large as my little finger. The details of this affair are as follows: Mr. Covey sent me, very early in the morning of one of our coldest days in the month of January, to the woods, to get a load of wood. He gave me a team of unbroken oxen. He told me which was the in-hand ox, and which the off-hand one. He then tied the end of a large rope around the horns of the in-hand ox, and gave me the other end of it, and told me, if the oxen started to run, that I must hold on upon the rope. I had never driven oxen before, and of course I was very awkward. I, however, succeeded in getting to the edge of the woods with little difficulty; but I had got a very few rods into the woods, when the oxen took fright, and started full tilt, carrying the cart against trees, and over stumps, in the most frightful manner. I expected every moment that my brains would be dashed out against the trees. After running thus for a considerable distance, they finally upset the cart, dashing it with great force against a tree, and threw themselves into a dense thicket. How I escaped death, I do not know. There I was, entirely alone, in a thick wood, in a place new to me. My cart was upset and shattered, my oxen were entangled among the young trees, and there was none to help me. After a long spell of effort, I succeeded in getting my cart righted, my oxen disentangled, and again yoked to the cart. I now proceeded with my team to the place where I had, the day before, been chopping wood, and loaded my cart pretty heavily, thinking in this way to tame my oxen. I then proceeded on my way home. I had now consumed one half of the day. I got out of the woods safely, and now felt out of danger. I stopped my oxen to open the woods gate; and just as I did so, before I could get hold of my ox-rope, the oxen again started, rushed through the gate, catching it between the wheel and the body of the cart, tearing it to pieces, and coming within a few inches of crushing me against the gate-post. Thus twice, in one short day, I escaped death by the merest chance. On my return, I told Mr. Covey what had happened, and how it happened. He ordered me to return to the woods again immediately. I did so, and he followed on after me. Just as I got into the woods, he came up and told me to stop my cart, and that he would teach me how to trifle away my time, and break gates. He then went to a large gum-tree, and with his axe cut three large switches, and, after trimming them up neatly with his pocket-knife, he ordered me to take off my clothes. I made him no answer, but stood with my clothes on. He repeated his order. I still made him no answer, nor did I move to strip myself. Upon this he rushed at me with the fierceness of a tiger, tore off my clothes, and lashed me till he had worn out his switches, cutting me so savagely as to leave the marks visible for a long time after. This whipping was the first of a number just like it, and for similar offences.

I lived with Mr. Covey one year. During the first six months, of that year, scarce a week passed without his whipping me. I was seldom free from a sore back. My awkwardness was almost always his excuse for whipping me. We were worked fully up to the point of endurance. Long before day we were up, our horses fed, and by the first approach of day we were off to the field with our hoes and ploughing teams. Mr. Covey gave us enough to eat, but scarce time to eat it. We were often less than five minutes taking our meals. We were often in the field from the first approach of day till its last lingering ray had left us; and at saving-fodder time,* midnight often caught us in the field binding blades.*

Covey would be out with us. The way he used to stand it, was this. He would spend the most of his afternoons in bed. He would then come out fresh in the evening, ready to urge us on with his words, example, and frequently with the whip. Mr. Covey was one of the few slaveholders who could and did work with his hands. He was a hard-working man. He knew by himself just what a man or a boy could do. There was no deceiving him. His work went on in his absence almost as well as in his presence; and he had the faculty of making us feel that he was ever present with us. This he did by surprising us. He seldom approached the spot where we were at work openly, if he could do it secretly. He always aimed at taking us by surprise. Such was his cunning, that we used to call him, among ourselves, "the snake." When we were at work in the cornfield, he would sometimes crawl on his hands and knees to avoid detection, and all at once he would rise nearly in our midst, and scream out, "Ha, ha! Come, come! Dash on, dash on!" This being his mode of attack, it was never safe to stop a single minute. His comings were like a thief in the night.* He appeared to us as being ever at hand. He was under every tree, behind every stump, in every bush, and at every window, on the plantation. He would sometimes mount his horse, as if bound to St. Michael's, a distance of seven miles, and in half an hour afterwards you would see him coiled up in the corner of the wood-fence, watching every motion of the slaves. He would, for this purpose, leave his horse tied up in the woods. Again, he would sometimes walk up to us, and give us orders as though he was upon the point of starting on a long journey, turn his back upon us, and make as though he was going to the house to get ready; and, before he would get half way thither, he would turn short and crawl into a fence-corner, or behind some tree, and there watch us till the going down of the sun.

Mr. Covey's *forte* consisted in his power to deceive. His life was devoted to planning and perpetrating the grossest deceptions. Every thing he possessed in the shape of learning or religion, he made conform to his disposition to deceive. He seemed to think himself equal to deceiving the Almighty. He would make a short prayer in the morning, and a long prayer at night; and, strange as it may seem, few men would at times appear more devotional than he. The exercises of his family devotions were always commenced with singing; and, as he was a very poor singer himself, the duty of raising the hymn generally came upon me. He would read his hymn, and nod at me to commence. I would at times do so; at others, I would not. My non-compliance would almost always produce much confusion. To show himself independent of me, he would start and stagger through with his hymn in the most discordant manner. In this state of mind, he prayed with more than ordinary spirit. Poor man! such was his disposition, and success at deceiving, I do verily believe that he sometimes deceived himself into the solemn belief, that he was a sincere worshipper of the most high God; and this, too, at a time when he may be said to have been guilty of compelling his woman slave to commit the sin of adultery. The facts in the case are these: Mr. Covey was a poor man; he was just commencing in life; he was only able to buy one slave; and, shocking as is the fact, he bought her, as he said, for *a breeder*. This woman was named Caroline. Mr. Covey bought her from Mr. Thomas Lowe, about six miles from St. Michael's. She was a large, able-bodied woman, about twenty years old. She had already given birth to one child, which proved her to be just what he wanted. After buying her, he hired a married man of Mr. Samuel Harrison, to live with him one year; and him he used to fasten up with her every night! The result was, that, at the end of the year, the miserable woman gave birth to twins. At this result Mr. Covey seemed to be highly pleased, both with the man and the wretched woman. Such was his joy, and that of his wife, that nothing they could do for Caroline during her confinement was too good, or too hard, to be done. The children were regarded as being quite an addition to his wealth.

If at any one time of my life more than another, I was made to drink the bitterest dregs of slavery, that time was during the first six months of my stay with Mr. Covey. We were worked in all weathers. It was never too hot or too cold; it could never rain, blow, hail, or snow, too hard for us to work in the field. Work, work, work, was scarcely more the order of the day than of the night. The longest days were too short for him, and the shortest nights too long for him. I was somewhat unmanageable when I first went there, but a few months of this discipline tamed me. Mr. Covey succeeded in breaking me. I was broken in body, soul, and spirit. My natural elasticity was crushed, my intellect languished, the disposition to read departed, the cheerful spark that lingered about my eye died; the dark night of slavery closed in upon me; and behold a man transformed into a brute!

Sunday was my only leisure time. I spent this in a sort of beast-like stupor, between sleep and wake, under some large tree. At times I would rise up, a flash of energetic freedom would dart through my soul, accompanied with a faint beam of hope, that flickered for a moment, and then vanished. I sank down again, mourning over my wretched condition. I was sometimes prompted to take my life, and that of Covey, but was prevented by a combination of hope and fear. My sufferings on this plantation seem now like a dream rather than a stern reality.

Our house stood within a few rods of the Chesapeake Bay, whose broad bosom was ever white with sails from every quarter of the habitable globe. Those beautiful vessels, robed in purest white, so delightful to the eye of freemen, were to me so many shrouded ghosts, to terrify and torment me with thoughts of my wretched condition. I have often, in the deep stillness of a summer's Sabbath, stood all alone upon the lofty banks of that noble bay, and traced, with saddened heart and tearful eye, the countless number of sails moving off to the mighty ocean. The sight of these always affected me powerfully. My thoughts would compel utterance; and there, with no audience but the Almighty, I would pour out my soul's complaint, in my rude way, with an apostrophe to the moving multitude of ships:—

"You are loosed from your moorings, and are free; I am fast in my chains, and am a slave! You move merrily before the gentle gale, and I sadly before the bloody whip! You are freedom's swift-winged angels, that fly round the world; I am confined in bands of iron! O that I were free! O, that I were on one of your gallant decks, and under your protecting wing! Alas! betwixt me and you, the turbid waters roll. Go on, go on. O, that I could also go! Could I but swim! If I could fly! O, why was I born a man, of whom to make a brute! The glad ship is gone; she hides in the dim distance. I am left in the hottest hell of unending slavery. O God, save me! God, deliver me! Let me be free! Is there any God! Why am I a slave? I will run away. I will not stand it. Get caught, or get clear, I'll try it. I had as well die with ague as the fever. I have only one life to lose. I had as well be killed running as die standing. Only think of it; one hundred miles straight north, and I am free! Try it? Yes! God helping me, I will. It cannot be that I shall live and die a slave. I will take to the water. This very bay shall yet bear me into freedom. The steamboats steered in a north-east course from North Point. I will do the same; and when I get to the head of the bay, I will turn my canoe adrift, and walk straight through Delaware into Pennsylvania. When I get there, I shall not be required to have a pass; I can travel without being disturbed. Let but the first opportunity offer, and, come what will, I am off. Meanwhile, I will try to bear up under the yoke. I am not the only slave in the world. Why should I fret? I can bear as much as any of them. Besides, I am but a boy, and all boys are bound to some one. It may be that my misery in slavery will only increase my happiness when I get free. There is a better day coming."

Thus I used to think, and thus I used to speak to myself; goaded almost to madness at one moment, and at the next reconciling myself to my wretched lot.

I have already intimated that my condition was much worse, during the first six months of my stay at Mr. Covey's, than in the last six. The circumstances leading to the change in Mr. Covey's course toward me form an epoch in my humble history. You have seen how a man was made a slave; you shall see how a slave was made a man. On one of the hottest days of the month of August, 1833, Bill Smith, William Hughes, a slave named Eli, and myself, were engaged in fanning wheat. Hughes was clearing the fanned wheat from before the fan,* Eli was turning, Smith was feeding, and I was carrying wheat to the fan. The work was simple, requiring strength rather than intellect; yet, to one entirely unused to such work, it came very hard. About three o'clock of that day, I broke down; my strength failed me; I was seized with a violent aching of the head, attended with extreme dizziness; I trembled in every limb. Finding what was coming, I nerved myself up, feeling it would never do to stop work. I stood as long as I could stagger to the hopper with grain. When I could stand no longer, I fell, and felt as if held down by an immense weight. The fan of course stopped; every one had his own work to do; and no one could do the work of the other, and have his own go on at the same time.

Mr. Covey was at the house, about one hundred yards from the treading-yard where we were fanning. On hearing the fan stop, he left immediately, and came to the spot where we were. He hastily inquired what the matter was. Bill answered that I was sick, and there was no one to bring wheat to the fan. I had by this time crawled away under the side of the post and rail-fence by which the yard was enclosed, hoping to find relief by getting out of the sun. He then asked where I was. He was told by one of the hands. He came to the spot, and, after looking at me awhile, asked me what was the matter. I told him as well as I could, for I scarce had strength to speak. He then gave me a savage kick in the side, and told me to get up. I tried to do so, but fell back in the attempt. He gave me another kick, and again told me to rise. I again tried, and succeeded in gaining my feet; but, stooping to get the tub with which I was feeding the fan, I again staggered and fell. While down in this situation, Mr. Covey took up the hickory slat with which Hughes had been striking off the half-bushel measure, and with it gave me a heavy blow upon the head, making a large wound, and the blood ran freely; and with this again told me to get up. I made no effort to comply, having now made up my mind to let him do his worst. In a short time after receiving this blow, my head grew better. Mr. Covey had now left me to my fate. At this moment I resolved, for the first time, to go to my master, enter a complaint, and ask his protection. In order to [do] this, I must that afternoon walk seven miles; and this, under the circumstances, was truly a severe undertaking. I was exceedingly feeble; made so as much by the kicks and blows which I received, as by the severe fit of sickness to which I had been subjected. I, however, watched my chance, while Covey was looking in an opposite direction, and started for St. Michael's. I succeeded in getting a considerable distance on my way to the woods, when Covey discovered me, and called after me to come back, threatening what he would do if I did not come. I disregarded both his calls and his threats, and made my way to the woods as fast as my feeble state would allow; and thinking I might be overhauled by him if I kept the road, I walked through the woods, keeping far enough from the road to avoid detection, and near enough to prevent losing my way. I had not gone far before my little strength again failed me. I could go no farther. I fell down, and lay for a considerable time. The blood was yet oozing from the wound on my head. For a time I thought I should bleed to death; and think now that I should have done so, but that the blood so matted my hair as to stop the wound. After lying there about three quarters of an hour, I nerved myself up again, and started on my way, through bogs and briers, bare-footed and bareheaded, tearing my feet sometimes at nearly every step; and after a journey of about seven miles, occupying some five hours to perform it, I arrived at master's store. I then presented an appearance enough to affect any but a heart of iron. From the crown of my head to my feet, I was covered with blood. My hair was all clotted with dust and blood; my shirt was stiff with blood. My legs and feet were torn in sundry places with briers and thorns, and were also covered with blood. I suppose I looked like a man who had escaped a den of wild beasts, and barely escaped them. In this state I appeared before my master, humbly entreating him to interpose his authority for my protection. I told him all the circumstances as well as I could, and it seemed, as I spoke, at times to affect him. He would then walk the floor, and seek to justify Covey by saying he expected I deserved it. He asked me what I wanted. I told him, to let me get a new home; that as sure as I lived with Mr. Covey again, I should live with but to die with him; that Covey would surely kill me; he was in a fair way for it. Master Thomas ridiculed the idea that there was any danger of Mr. Covey's killing me, and said that he knew Mr. Covey; that he was a good man, and that he could not think of taking me from him; that, should he do so, he would lose the whole year's wages; that I belonged to Mr. Covey for one year, and that I must go back to him, come what might; and that I must not trouble him with any more stories, or that he would himself *get hold of me*. After threatening me thus, he gave me a very large dose of salts, telling me that I might remain in St.

Michael's that night, (it being quite late,) but that I must be off back to Mr. Covey's early in the morning; and that if I did not, he would *get hold of me*, which meant that he would whip me. I remained all night, and, according to his orders, I started off to Covey's in the morning, (Saturday morning,) wearied in body and broken in spirit. I got no supper that night, or breakfast that morning. I reached Covey's about nine o'clock; and just as I was getting over the fence that divided Mrs. Kemp's fields from ours, out ran Covey with his cowskin, to give me another whipping. Before he could reach me, I succeeded in getting to the cornfield; and as the corn was very high, it afforded me the means of hiding. He seemed very angry, and searched for me a long time. My behavior was altogether unaccountable. He finally gave up the chase, thinking, I suppose, that I must come home for something to eat; he would give himself no further trouble in looking for me. I spent that day mostly in the woods, having the alternative before me,—to go home and be whipped to death, or stay in the woods and be starved to death. That night, I fell in with Sandy Jenkins, a slave with whom I was somewhat acquainted. Sandy had a free wife, who lived about four miles from Mr. Covey's; and it being Saturday, he was on his way to see her. I told him my circumstances, and he very kindly invited me to go home with him. I went home with him, and talked this whole matter over, and got his advice as to what course it was best for me to pursue. I found Sandy an old adviser. He told me, with great solemnity, I must go back to Covey; but that before I went, I must go with him into another part of the woods, where there was a certain *root*, which, if I would take some of it with me, carrying it *always on my right side*, would render it impossible for Mr. Covey, or any other white man, to whip me. He said he had carried it for years; and since he had done so, he had never received a blow, and never expected to while he carried it. I at first rejected the idea, that the simple carrying of a root in my pocket would have any such effect as he had said, and was not disposed to take it; but Sandy impressed the necessity with much earnestness, telling me it could do no harm, if it did no good. To please him, I at length took the root, and, according to his direction, carried it upon my right side. This was Sunday morning. I immediately started for home; and upon entering the yard gate, out came Mr. Covey on his way to meeting. He spoke to me very kindly, bade me drive the pigs from a lot near by, and passed on towards the church. Now, this singular conduct of Mr. Covey really made me begin to think that there was something in the *root* which Sandy had given me; and had it been on any other day than Sunday, I could have attributed the conduct to no other cause than the influence of that root; and as it was, I was half inclined to think the *root* to be something more than I at first had taken it to be. All went well till Monday morning. On this morning, the virtue of the *root* was fully tested. Long before daylight, I was called to go and rub, curry, and feed, the horses. I obeyed, and was glad to obey. But whilst thus engaged, whilst in the act of throwing down some blades from the loft, Mr. Covey entered the stable with a long rope; and just as I was half out of the loft, he caught hold of my legs, and was about tying me. As soon as I found what he was up to, I gave a sudden spring, and as I did so, he holding to my legs, I was brought sprawling on the stable floor. Mr. Covey seemed now to think he had me, and could do what he pleased; but at this moment—from whence came the spirit I don't know—I resolved to fight; and, suiting my action to the resolution, I seized Covey hard by the throat; and as I did so, I rose. He held on to me, and I to him. My resistance was so entirely unexpected, that Covey seemed taken all aback. He trembled like a leaf. This gave me assurance, and I held him uneasy, causing the blood to run where I touched him with the ends of my fingers. Mr. Covey soon called out to Hughes for help. Hughes came, and, while Covey held me, attempted to tie my right hand. While he was in the act of doing so, I watched my chance, and gave him a heavy kick close under the ribs. This kick fairly sickened Hughes, so that he left me in the hands of Mr. Covey. This kick had the effect of not only weakening Hughes, but Covey also. When he saw Hughes bending over with pain, his courage quailed. He asked me if I meant to persist in my resistance. I told him I did, come what might; that he had used me like a brute for six months, and that I was determined to be used so no longer. With that, he strove to drag me to a stick that was lying just out of the stable door. He meant to knock me down. But just as he was leaning over to get the stick, I seized him with both hands by his collar, and brought him by a sudden snatch to the ground. By this time, Bill came. Covey called upon him for assistance. Bill wanted to know what he could do. Covey said, "Take hold of him, take hold of him!" Bill said his master hired him out to work, and not to help to whip me; so he left Covey and myself to fight our own battle out. We were at it for nearly two hours. Covey at length let me go, puffing and blowing at a great rate, saying that if I had not resisted, he would not have whipped me half so much. The truth was, that he had not whipped me at all. I considered him as getting entirely the worst end of the bargain; for he had drawn no blood from me, but I had from him. The whole six months afterwards, that I spent with Mr. Covey, he never laid the weight of his finger upon me in anger. He would occasionally say, he didn't want to get hold of me again. "No," thought I, "you need not; for you will come off worse than you did before."

This battle with Mr. Covey was the turning-point in my career as a slave. It rekindled the few expiring embers of freedom, and revived within me a sense of my own manhood. It recalled the departed self-confidence, and inspired me again with a determination to be free. The gratification afforded by the triumph was a full compensation for whatever else might follow, even death itself. He only can understand the deep satisfaction which I experience, who has himself repelled by force the bloody arm of slavery. I felt as I never felt before. It was a glorious resurrection, for the tomb of slavery, to the heaven of freedom. My long-crushed spirit rose, cowardice departed, bold defiance took its place; and I now resolved that, however long I might remain a slave in form, the day has passed forever when I could be a slave in fact. I did not hesitate to let it be known of me, that the white man who expected to succeed in whipping, must also succeed in killing me.

From this time I was never again what might be called fairly whipped, though I remained a slave four years afterwards. I had several fights, but was never whipped.

It was for a long time a matter of surprise to me why Mr. Covey did not immediately have me taken by the constable to the whipping-post, and there regularly whipped for the crime of raising my hand against a white man in defence of myself. And the only explanation I can now think of does not entirely satisfy me; but such as it is, I will give it. Mr. Covey enjoyed the most unbounded reputation for being a first-rate overseer and negro-breaker. It was of considerable importance to him. That reputation was at stake; and had he sent me—a boy about sixteen years old—to the public whipping-post, his reputation would have been lost; so, to save his reputation, he suffered me to go unpunished.

My term of actual service to Mr. Edward Covey ended on Christmas day, 1833. The days between Christmas and New Year's day are allowed as holidays; and, accordingly, we were not required to perform any labor, more than to feed and take care of the stock. This time we regarded as our own, by the grace of our masters; and we therefore used or abused it nearly as we pleased. Those of us who had families at a distance, were generally allowed to spend the whole six days in their society. This time, however, was spent in various ways. The staid, sober, thinking and industrious ones of our number would employ themselves in making corn-brooms, mats, horse-collars, and baskets; and another class of us would spend the time in hunting opossums, hares, and coons. But by far the larger part engaged in such sports and merriments as playing ball, wrestling, running foot-races, fiddling, dancing, and drinking whisky; and this latter mode of spending the time was by far the most agreeable to the feelings of our masters. A slave who would work during the holidays was considered by our masters as scarcely deserving them. He was regarded as one who rejected the favor of his master. It was deemed a disgrace not to get drunk at Christmas; and he was regarded as lazy indeed, who had not provided himself with the necessary means, during the year, to get whisky enough to last him through Christmas.

From what I know of the effect of these holidays upon the slave, I believe them to be among the most effective means in the hands of the slaveholder in keeping down the spirit of insurrection. Were the slaveholders at once to abandon this practice, I have not the slightest doubt it would lead to an immediate insurrection among the slaves. These holidays serve as conductors, or safety-valves, to carry off the rebellious spirit of enslaved humanity. But for these, the slave would be forced up to the wildest desperation; and woe betide the slaveholder, the day he ventures to remove or hinder the operation of those conductors! I warn him that, in such an event, a spirit will go forth in their midst, more to be dreaded than the most appalling earthquake.

The holidays are part and parcel of the gross fraud, wrong, and inhumanity of slavery. They are professedly a custom established by the benevolence of the slaveholders; but I undertake to say, it is the result of selfishness, and one of the grossest frauds committed upon the down-trodden slave. They do not give the slaves this time because they would not like to have their work during its continuance, but because they know it would be unsafe to deprive them of it. This will be seen by the fact, that the slaveholders like to have their slaves spend those days just in such a manner as to make them as glad of their ending as of their beginning. Their object seems to be, to disgust their slaves with freedom, by plunging them into the lowest depths of dissipation. For instance, the slaveholders not only like to see the slave drink of his own accord, but will adopt various plans to make him drunk. One plan is, to make bets on their slaves, as to who can drink the most whisky without getting drunk; and in this way they succeed in getting whole multitudes to drink to excess. Thus, when the slave asks for virtuous freedom, the cunning slaveholder, knowing his ignorance, cheats him with a dose of vicious dissipation, artfully labelled with the name of liberty. The most of us used to drink it down, and the result was just what might be supposed: many of us were led to think that there was little to choose between liberty and slavery. We felt, and very properly too, that we had almost as well be slaves to man as to rum. So, when the holidays ended, we staggered up from the filth of our wallowing, took a long breath, and marched to the field,—feeling, upon the whole, rather glad to go, from what our master had deceived us into a belief was freedom, back to the arms of slavery.

I have said that this mode of treatment is a part of the whole system of fraud and inhumanity of slavery. It is so. The mode here adopted to disgust the slave with freedom, by allowing him to see only the abuse of it, is carried out in other things. For instance, a slave loves molasses; he steals some. His master, in many cases, goes off to town, and buys a large quantity; he returns, takes his whip, and commands the slave to eat the molasses, until the poor fellow is made sick at the very mention of it. The same mode is sometimes adopted to make the slaves refrain from asking for more food than their regular allowance. A slave runs through his allowance, and applies for more. His master is enraged at him; but, not willing to send him off without food, gives him more than is necessary, and compels him to eat it within a given time. Then, if he complains that he cannot eat it, he is said to be satisfied neither full nor fasting, and is whipped for being hard to please! I have an abundance of such illustrations of the same principle, drawn from my own observation, but think the cases I have cited sufficient. The practice is a very common one.

On the first of January, 1834, I left Mr. Covey, and went to live with Mr. William Freeland, who lived about three miles from St. Michael's. I soon found Mr. Freeland a very different man from Mr. Covey. Though not rich, he was what would be called an educated southern gentleman. Mr. Covey, as I have shown, was a well-trained negro-breaker and slave-driver. The former (slaveholder though he was) seemed to possess some regard for honor, some reverence for justice, and some respect for humanity. The latter seemed totally insensible to all such sentiments. Mr. Freeland had many of the faults peculiar to slaveholders, such as being very passionate and fretful; but I must do him the justice to say, that he was exceedingly free from those degrading vices to which Mr. Covey was constantly addicted. The one was open and frank, and we always knew where to find him. The other was a most artful deceiver, and could be understood only by such as were skilful enough to detect his cunningly-devised frauds. Another advantage I gained in my new master was, he made no pretensions to, or profession of, religion; and this, in my opinion, was truly a great advantage. I assert most unhesitatingly, that the religion of the south is a mere covering for the most horrid crimes,—a justifier of the most appalling barbarity,—a sanctifier of the most hateful frauds,—and a dark shelter under, which the darkest, foulest, grossest, and most infernal deeds of slaveholders find the strongest protection. Were I to be again reduced to the chains of slavery, next to that enslavement, I should regard being the slave of a religious master the greatest calamity that could befall me. For of all slaveholders with whom I have ever met, religious slaveholders are the worst. I have ever found them the meanest and basest, and most cruel and cowardly, of all others. It was my unhappy lot not only to belong to a religious slaveholder, but to live in a community of such religionists. Very near Mr. Freeland lived the Rev. Daniel Weeden, and in the same neighborhood lived the Rev. Rigby Hopkins. These were members and ministers in the Reformed Methodist Church. Mr. Weeden owned, among others, a woman slave, whose name I have forgotten. This woman's back, for weeks, was kept literally raw, made so by the lash of this merciless, *religious* wretch. He used to hire hands. His maxim was, Behave well or behave ill, it is the duty of a master occasionally to whip a slave, to remind him of his master's authority. Such was his theory, and such his practice.

Mr. Hopkins was even worse than Mr. Weeden. His chief boast was his ability to manage slaves. The peculiar feature of his government was that of whipping slaves in advance of deserving it. He always managed to have one or more of his slaves to whip every Monday morning. He did this to alarm their fears, and strike terror into those who escaped. His plan was to whip for the smallest offences, to prevent the commission of large ones. Mr. Hopkins could always find some excuse for whipping a slave. It would astonish one, unaccustomed to a slaveholding life, to see with what wonderful ease a slaveholder can find things, of which to make occasion to whip a slave. A mere look, word, or motion,—a mistake, accident, or want of power,—are all matters for which a slave may be whipped at any time. Does a slave look dissatisfied? It is said, he has the devil in him, and it must be whipped out. Does he speak loudly when spoken to by his master? Then he is getting high-minded, and should be taken down a buttonhole lower. Does he forget to pull off his hat at the approach of a white person? Then he is wanting in reverence, and should be whipped for it. Does he ever venture to vindicate his conduct, when censured for it? Then he is guilty of im-pudence,—one of the greatest crimes of which a slave can be guilty. Does he ever venture to suggest a different mode of doing things from that pointed out by his master? He is indeed pre-sumptuous, and getting above himself; and nothing less than a flogging will do for him. Does he, while ploughing, break a plough,—or, while hoeing, break a hoe? It is owning to his care-lessness, and for it a slave must always be whipped. Mr. Hopkins could always find something of this sort to justify the use of the lash, and he seldom, failed to embrace such opportunities. There was not a man in the whole county, with whom the slaves who had the getting their own home, would not prefer to live, rather than with this Rev. Mr. Hopkins. And yet there was not a man any where round, who made higher professions of religion, or was more active in revivals,—more attentive to the class, love-feast, prayer and preaching meetings, or more devotional in his family,—that prayed earlier, later, louder, and longer,—than this same reverend slave-driver, Rigby Hopkins.

But to return to Mr. Freeland, and to my experience while in his employment. He, like Mr. Covey, gave us enough to eat; but, unlike Mr. Covey, he also gave us sufficient time to take our meals. He worked us hard, but always between sunrise and sun-set. He required a good deal of work to be done, but gave us good tools with which to work. His farm was large, but he employed hands enough to work it, and with ease, compared with many of his neighbors. My treatment, while in his employment, was heavenly, compared with what I experienced at the hands of Mr. Edward Covey.

Mr. Freeland was himself the owner of but two slaves. Their names were Henry Harris and John Harris. The rest of his hands he hired. These consisted of myself, Sandy Jenkins,[1] and Handy Caldwell. Henry and John were quite intelligent, and in a very little while after I went there, I succeeded in creating in them a strong desire to learn how to read. This desire soon sprang up in the others also. They very soon mustered up some old spelling-books, and nothing would do but that I must keep a Sabbath school. I agreed to do so, and accordingly devoted my Sundays to teaching these my loved fellow-slaves how to read. Neither of them knew his letters when I went there. Some of the slaves of the neighboring farms found what was going on; and also availed themselves of this little opportunity to learn to read. It was understood, among all who came, that there must be as little display about it as possible. It was necessary to keep our religious masters at St. Michael's unacquainted with the fact, that, instead of spending the Sabbath in wrestling, boxing, and drinking whisky, we were trying to learn how to read the will of God; for they had much rather see us engaged in those degrading sports, than to see us behaving like intellectual, moral, and accountable beings. My blood boils as I think of the bloody manner in which Messrs. Wright Fairbanks and Garrison West, both class-leaders, in connection with many others, rushed in upon us with sticks and stones, and broke up our virtuous little Sabbath school, at St. Michael's—all calling themselves Christians! humble followers of the Lord Jesus Christ! But I am again digressing.

I held my Sabbath school at the house of a free colored man, whose name I deem it imprudent to mention; for should it be known, it might embarrass him greatly, though the crime of holding the school was committed ten years ago. I had at one time over forty scholars, and those of the right sort, ardently desiring to learn. They were of all ages, though mostly men and women. I

---

[1] This is the same man who gave me the roots to prevent my being whipped by Mr. Covey. He was "a clever soul." We used frequently to talk about the fight with Covey, and as often as we did so, he would claim my success as the result of the roots which he gave me. This superstition is very common among the more ignorant slaves. A slave seldom dies but this his death is attributed to trickery. [Douglass's note]

look back to those Sundays with an amount of pleasure not to be expressed. They were great days to my soul. The work of instructing my dear fellow-slaves was the sweetest engagement with which I was ever blessed. We loved each other, and to leave them at the close of the Sabbath was a severe cross indeed. When I think that these precious souls are to-day shut up in the prison-house of slavery, my feelings overcome me, and I am almost ready to ask, "Does a righteous God govern the universe? and for what does he hold the thunders in his right hand, if not to smite the oppressor, and deliver the spoiled out of the hand of the spoiler?" These dear souls came not to Sabbath school because it was popular to do so, nor did I teach them because it was reputable to be thus engaged. Every moment they spent in that school, they were liable to be taken up, and given thirty-nine lashes. They came because they wished to learn. Their minds had been starved by their cruel masters. They had been shut up in mental darkness. I taught them, because it was the delight of my soul to be doing something that looked like bettering the condition of my race. I kept up my school nearly the whole year I lived with Mr. Freeland; and, beside my Sabbath school, I devoted three evenings in the week, during the winter, to teaching the slaves at home. And I have the happiness to know, that several of those who came to Sabbath school learned how to read; and that one, at least, is now free through my agency.

The year passed off smoothly. It seemed only about half as long as the year which preceded it. I went through it without receiving a single blow. I will give Mr. Freeland the credit of being the best master I ever had, *till I became my own master.* For the ease with which I passed the year, I was, however, somewhat indebted to the society of my fellow-slaves. They were noble souls; they not only possessed loving hearts, but brave ones. We were linked and interlinked with each other. I loved them with a love stronger than any thing I have experienced since. It is some-times said that we slaves do not love and confide in each other. In answer to this assertion, I can say, I never loved any or confided in any people more than my fellow-slaves, and especially those with whom I lived at Mr. Freeland's. I believe we would have died for each other. We never undertook to do any thing, of any importance, without a mutual consultation. We never moved separately. We were one; and as much so by our tempers and dispositions, as by the mutual hardships to which we were necessarily subjected by our condition as slaves.

At the close of the year 1834, Mr. Freeland again hired me of my master, for the year 1835. But, by this time, I began to want to live *upon free land* as well as *with Freeland;* and I was no longer content, therefore, to live with him or any other slaveholder. I began, with the commencement of the year, to prepare myself for a final struggle, which should decide my fate one way or the other. My tendency was upward. I was fast approaching manhood, and year after year had passed, and I was still a slave. These thoughts roused me—I must do something. I therefore resolved that 1835 should not pass without witnessing an attempt, on my part, to secure my liberty. But I was not willing to cherish this determination alone. My fellow-slaves were dear to me. I was anxious to have them participate with me in this, my life-giving determination. I therefore, though with great prudence, commenced early to ascertain their views and feelings in regard to their condition, and to imbue their minds with thoughts of freedom. I bent myself to devising ways and means for our escape, and meanwhile strove, on all fitting occasions, to impress them with the gross fraud and inhumanity of slavery. I went first to Henry, next to John, then to the others. I found, in them all, warm hearts and noble spirits. They were ready to hear, and ready to act when a feasible plan should be proposed. This was what I wanted. I talked to them of our want of manhood, if we submitted to our enslavement without at least one noble effort to be free. We met often, and consulted frequently, and told our hopes and fears, recounted the difficulties, real and imagined, which we should be called on to meet. At times we were almost disposed to give up, and try to content ourselves with our wretched lot; at others, we were firm and unbending in our determination to go. Whenever we suggested any plan, there was shrinking—the odds were fearful. Our path was beset with the greatest obstacles; and if we succeeded in gaining the end of it, our right to be free was yet questionable—we were yet liable to be returned to bondage. We could see no spot, this side of the ocean, where we could be free. We knew nothing about Canada. Our knowledge of the north did not extend farther than New York; and to go there, and be forever harassed with the frightful liability of being returned to slavery—with the certainty of being treated tenfold worse than before—the thought was truly a horrible one, and one which it was not easy to overcome. The case sometimes stood thus: At every gate through which we were to pass, we saw a watchman— at every ferry a guard—on every bridge a sentinel—and in every wood a patrol. We were hemmed in upon every side. Here were the difficulties, real or imagined—the good to be sought, and the evil to be shunned. On the one hand, there stood slavery, a stern reality, glaring frightfully upon us,—its robes already crimsoned with the blood of millions, and even now feasting itself greedily upon our own flesh. On the other hand, away back in the dim distance, under the flickering light of the north star, behind some craggy hill or snow-covered mountain, stood a doubtful freedom—half frozen—beckoning us to come and share its hospitality. This in itself was sometimes enough to stagger us; but when we permitted ourselves to survey the road, we were frequently appalled. Upon either side we saw grim death, assuming the most horrid shapes. Now it was starvation; causing us to eat our own flesh;—now we were contending with the waves, and were drowned;—now we were overtaken, and torn to pieces by the fangs of the terrible bloodhound. We were stung by scorpions, chased by wild beasts, bitten by snakes, and finally, after having nearly reached the desired spot,—after swimming rivers, encountering wild beasts, sleeping in the woods, suffering hunger and nakedness,—we were overtaken by our pursuers, and, in our resistance, we were shot dead upon the spot! I say, this picture sometimes appalled us, and made us

> "rather bear those ills we had,
> Than fly to others, that we knew not of."*

In coming to a fixed determination to run away, we did more than Patrick Henry, when he resolved upon liberty or death. With us it was a doubtful liberty at most, and almost certain death if we failed. For my part, I should prefer death to hopeless bondage.

Sandy, one of our number, gave up the notion, but still encouraged us. Our company then consisted of Henry Harris, John Harris, Henry Bailey, Charles Roberts, and myself. Henry Bailey was my uncle, and belonged to my master. Charles married my aunt; he belonged to my master's father-in-law, Mr. William Hamilton.

The plan we finally concluded upon was, to get a large canoe belonging to Mr. Hamilton, and upon the Saturday night previous to Easter holidays, paddle directly up the Chesapeake Bay. On our arrival at the head of the bay, a distance of seventy or eighty miles from where we lived, it was our purpose to turn our canoe adrift, and follow the guidance of the north star till we got beyond the limits of Maryland. Our reason for taking the water route was, that we were less liable to be suspected as runaways; we hoped to be regarded as fishermen; whereas, if we should take the land route, we should be subjected to interruptions of almost every kind. Any one having a white face, and being so disposed, could stop us, and subject us to examination.

The week before our intended start, I wrote several protections, one for each of us. As well as I can remember, they were in the following words, to wit:—

"THIS is to certify that I, the undersigned, have given the bearer, my servant, full liberty to go to Baltimore, and spend the Easter holidays. Written with mine own hand, &c., 1835.

"WILLIAM HAMILTON,
"Near St. Michael's, in Talbot county, Maryland."

We were not going to Baltimore; but, in going up the bay, we went toward Baltimore, and these protections were only intended to protect us while on the bay.

As the time drew near for our departure, our anxiety became more and more intense. It was truly a matter of life and death with us. The strength of our determination was about to be fully tested. At this time, I was very active in explaining every difficulty, removing every doubt, dispelling every fear, and inspiring all with the firmness indispensable to success in our undertaking; assuring them that half was gained the instant we made the move; we had talked long enough; we were now ready to move; if not now, we never should be, and if we did not intend to move now, we had as well fold our arms, sit down, and acknowledge ourselves fit only to be slaves. This, none of us were prepared to acknowledge. Every man stood firm; and at our last meeting, we pledged ourselves afresh, in the most solemn manner, that, at the time appointed, we would certainly start in pursuit of freedom. This was in the middle of the week, at the end of which we were to be off. We went, as usual, to our several fields of labor, but with bosoms highly agitated with thoughts of our truly hazardous undertaking. We tried to conceal our feelings as much as possible; and I think we succeeded very well.

After a painful waiting, the Saturday morning, whose night was to witness our departure, came. I hailed it with joy, bring what of sadness it might. Friday night was a sleepless one for me. I probably felt more anxious than the rest, because I was, by common consent, at the head of the whole affair. The responsibility of success or failure lay heavily upon me. The glory of the one, and the confusion of the other, were alike mine. The first two hours of that morning were such as I never experienced before, and hope never to again. Early in the morning; we went, as usual, to the field. We were spreading manure; and all at once, while thus engaged, I was overwhelmed with an indescribable feeling, in the fulness of which I turned to Sandy, who was near by, and said, "We are betrayed!" "Well," said he, "that thought has this moment struck me." We said no more. I was never more certain of any thing.

The horn was blown as usual, and we went up from the field to the house for breakfast. I went for the form, more than for want of any thing to eat that morning. Just as I got to the house, in looking out at the lane gate, I saw four white men, with two colored men. The white men were on horseback, and the colored ones were walking behind, as if tied. I watched them a few moments till they got up to our lane gate. Here they halted, and tied the colored men to the gatepost. I was not yet certain as to what the matter was. In a few moments, in rode Mr. Hamilton, with a speed betokening great excitement. He came to the door, and inquired if Master William was in. He was told he was at the barn. Mr. Hamilton, without dismounting, rode up to the barn with extraordinary speed. In a few moments, he and Mr. Freeland returned to the house. By this time, the three constables rode up, and in great haste dismounted, tied their horses, and met Master William and Mr. Hamilton returning from the barn; and after talking awhile, they all walked up to the kitchen door. There was no one in the kitchen but myself and John. Henry and Sandy were up at the barn. Mr. Freeland put his head in at the door, and called me by name, saying, there were some gentlemen at the door who wished to see me. I stepped to the door, and inquired what they wanted. They at once seized me, and, without giving me any satisfaction, tied me—lashing my hands closely together. I insisted upon knowing what the matter was. They at length said, that they had learned I had been in a "scrape," and that I was to be examined before my master; and if their information proved false, I should not be hurt.

In a few moments, they succeeded in tying John. They then turned to Henry, who had by this time returned, and commanded him to cross his hands. "I won't!" said Henry, in a firm tone, indicating his readiness to meet the consequences of his refusal. "Won't you?" said Tom Graham, the constable. "No, I won't!" said Henry, in a still stronger tone. With this, two of the constables pulled out their shining pistols, and swore, by their Creator, that they would make him cross his hands or kill him. Each cocked his pistol, and, with fingers on the trigger, walked up to Henry, saying, at the same time, if he did not cross his hands, they would blow his damned heart out. "Shoot me, shoot me!" said Henry; "you can't kill me but once. Shoot, shoot,—and be damned! *I won't be tied!*" This he said in a tone of loud defiance; and at the same time, with a motion as quick as lightning, he with one single stroke dashed the pistols from the hand of each constable. As he did this, all hands fell upon him, and, after beating him some time, they finally overpowered him, and got him tied.

During the scuffle, I managed, I know not how, to get my pass out, and, without being discovered, put it into the fire. We were all now tied; and just as we were to leave for Easton jail, Betsy Freeland, mother of William Freeland, came to the door with her hands full of biscuits, and divided them between Henry and John. She then delivered herself of a speech, to the following effect:— addressing herself to me, she said, "*You devil! You yellow devil!* it was you that put it into the heads of Henry and John to run away. But for you, you long-legged mulatto devil! Henry nor John would never have thought of such a thing." I made no reply, and was immediately hurried off towards St. Michael's. Just a moment previous to the scuffle with Henry, Mr. Hamilton suggested the propriety of making a search for the protections which he had understood Frederick had written for himself and the rest. But, just at the moment he was about carrying his proposal into effect, his aid was needed in helping to tie Henry; and the excitement attending the scuffle caused them either to forget, or to deem it unsafe, under the circumstances, to search. So we were not yet convicted of the intention to run away.

When we got about half way to St. Michael's, while the constables having us in charge were looking ahead, Henry inquired of me what he should do with his pass. I told him to eat it with his biscuit, and own nothing; and we passed the word around, "*Own nothing;*" and "*Own nothing!*" said we all. Our confidence in each other was unshaken. We were resolved to succeed or fail together, after the calamity had befallen us as much as before. We were now prepared for any thing. We were to be dragged that morning fifteen miles behind horses, and then to be placed in the Easton jail. When we reached St. Michael's, we underwent a sort of examination. We all denied that we ever intended to run away. We did this more to bring out the evidence against us, than from any hope of getting clear of being sold; for, as I have said, we were ready for that. The fact was, we cared but little where we went, so we went together. Our greatest concern was about separation. We dreaded that more than any thing this side of death. We found the evidence against us to be the testimony of one person; our master would not tell who it was; but we came to a unanimous decision among ourselves as to who their informant was. We were sent off to the jail at Easton. When we got there, we were delivered up to the sheriff, Mr. Joseph Graham, and by him placed in jail. Henry, John, and myself, were placed in one room together—Charles, and Henry Bailey, in another. Their object in separating us was to hinder concert.

We had been in jail scarcely twenty minutes, when a swarm of slave traders, and agents for slave traders, flocked into jail to look at us, and to ascertain if we were for sale. Such a set of beings I never saw before! I felt myself surrounded by so many fiends from perdition. A band of pirates never looked more like their father, the devil. They laughed and grinned over us, saying, "Ah, my boys! we have got you, haven't we?" And after taunting us in various ways, they one by one went into an examination of us, with intent to ascertain our value. They would impudently ask us if we would not like to have them for our masters. We would make them no answer, and leave them to find out as best they could. Then they would curse and swear at us, telling us that they could take the devil out of us in a very little while, if we were only in their hands.

While in jail, we found ourselves in much more comfortable quarters than we expected when we went there. We did not get much to eat, nor that which was very good; but we had a good clean room, from the windows of which we could see what was going on in the street, which was very much better than though we had been placed in one of the dark, damp cells. Upon the whole, we got along very well, so far as the jail and its keeper were concerned. Immediately after the holidays were over, contrary to all our expectations, Mr. Hamilton and Mr. Freeland came up to Easton, and took Charles, the two Henrys, and John, out of jail, and carried them home, leaving me alone. I regarded this separation as a final one. It caused me more pain than any thing else in the whole transaction. I was ready for any thing rather than separation. I supposed that they had consulted together, and had decided that, as I was the whole cause of the intention of the others to run away, it was hard to make the innocent suffer with the guilty; and that they had, therefore, concluded to take the others home, and sell me, as a warning to the others that remained. It is due to the noble Henry to say, he seemed almost as reluctant at leaving the prison as at leaving home to come to the prison. But we knew we should, in all probability, be separated, if we were sold; and since he was in their hands, he concluded to go peaceably home.

I was now left to my fate. I was all alone, and within the walls of a stone prison. But a few days before, and I was full of hope. I expected to have been safe in a land of freedom; but now I was covered with gloom, sunk down to the utmost despair. I thought the possibility of freedom was gone. I was kept in this way about one week, at the end of which, Captain Auld, my master, to my surprise and utter astonishment, came up, and took me out, with the intention of sending me, with a gentleman of his acquaintance, into Alabama. But, from some cause or other, he did not send me to Alabama, but concluded to send me back to Baltimore, to live again with his brother Hugh, and to learn a trade.

Thus, after an absence of three years and one month, I was once more permitted to return to my old home at Baltimore. My master sent me away, because there existed against me a very great prejudice in the community, and he feared I might be killed.

In a few weeks after I went to Baltimore, Master Hugh hired me to Mr. William Gardner, an extensive ship-builder, on Fell's Point. I was put there to learn how to calk. It, however, proved a very unfavorable place for the accomplishment of this object. Mr. Gardner was engaged that spring in building two large man-of-war brigs, professedly for the Mexican government. The vessels were to be launched in the July of that year, and in failure thereof, Mr. Gardner was to lose a considerable sum; so that when I entered, all was hurry. There was no time to learn any thing. Every man had to do that which he knew how to do. In entering the ship-yard, my orders from Mr. Gardner were, to do whatever the carpenters commanded me to do. This was placing me at the beck and call of about seventy-five men. I was to regard all these as masters. Their word was to be my law. My situation was a most trying one. At times I needed a dozen pair of hands. I was called a dozen ways in the space of a single minute. Three or four voices would strike my ear at the same moment. It was—"Fred., come help me to cant this timber here."—"Fred., come carry this timber yonder."—"Fred., bring that roller here."—"Fred., go get a fresh can of water."—"Fred., come help saw off the end of this timber."—"Fred., go quick, and get the crowbar."—"Fred., hold on the end of this fall."—"Fred., go to the blacksmith's shop, and get a new punch."—"Hurra, Fred.!* run and bring me a cold chisel."—"I say, Fred., bear a hand, and get up a fire as quick as lightning under that steam-box."—"Halloo, nigger! come, turn this grindstone."—"Come, come! move, move! and *bowse** this timber forward."—"I say, darky, blast your eyes, why don't you heat up some pitch?"—"Halloo! halloo! halloo!" (Three voices at the same time.) "Come here!—Go there!—Hold on where you are! Damn you, if you move, I'll knock your brains out!"

This was my school for eight months; and I might have remained there longer, but for a most horrid fight I had with four of the white apprentices, in which my left eye was nearly knocked out, and I was horribly mangled in other respects. The facts in the case were these: Until a very little while after I went there, white and black ship-carpenters worked side by side, and no one seemed to see any impropriety in it. All hands seemed to be very well satisfied. Many of the black carpenters were freemen. Things seemed to be going on very well. All at once, the white carpenters knocked off, and said they would not work with free colored workmen. Their reason for this, as alleged, was, that if free colored carpenters were encouraged, they would soon take the trade into their own hands, and poor white men would be thrown out of employment. They therefore felt called upon at once to put a stop to it. And, taking advantage of Mr. Gardner's necessities, they broke off, swearing they would work no longer, unless he would discharge his black carpenters. Now, though this did not extend to me in form, it did reach me in fact. My fellow-apprentices very soon began to feel it degrading to them to work with me. They began to put on airs, and talk about the "niggers" taking the country, saying we all ought to be killed; and, being encouraged by the journeymen, they commenced making my condition as hard as they could, by hectoring me around, and sometimes striking me. I, of course, kept the vow I made after the fight with Mr.

Covey, and struck back again, regardless of consequences; and
while I kept them from combining, I succeeded very well; for I
could whip the whole of them, taking them separately. They,
however, at length combined, and came upon me, armed with
sticks, stones, and heavy handspikes. One came in front with a
half brick. There was one at each side of me, and one behind me.
While I was attending to those in front, and on either side, the
one behind ran up with the handspike, and struck me a heavy
blow upon the head. It stunned me. I fell, and with this they all
ran upon me, and fell to beating me with their fists. I let them lay
on for a while, gathering strength. In an instant, I gave a sudden
surge, and rose to my hands and knees. Just as I did that, one of
their number gave me, with his heavy boot, a powerful kick in the
left eye. My eyeball seemed to have burst. When they saw my eye
closed, and badly swollen, they left me. With this I seized the
handspike, and for a time pursued them. But here the carpenters
interfered, and I thought I might as well give it up. It was impossible to stand my hand against so many. All this took place in sight
of not less than fifty white ship-carpenters, and not one inter-
posed a friendly word; but some cried, "Kill the damned nigger!
Kill him! kill him! He struck a white person." I found my only
chance for life was in flight. I succeeded in getting away without
an additional blow, and barely so; for to strike a white man is
death by Lynch law,—and that was the law in Mr. Gardner's
ship-yard; nor is there much of any other out of Mr. Gardner's
ship-yard.

I went directly home, and told the story of my wrongs to
Master Hugh; and I am happy to say of him, irreligious as he was,
his conduct was heavenly, compared with that of his brother
Thomas under similar circumstances. He listened attentively to
my narration of the circumstances leading to the savage outrage,
and gave many proofs of his strong indignation at it. The heart of
my once overkind mistress was again melted into pity. My
puffed-out eye and blood-covered face moved her to tears. She
took a chair by me, washed the blood from my face, and, with a
mother's tenderness, bound up my head, covering the wounded
eye with a lean piece of fresh beef. It was almost compensation

for my suffering to witness, once more, a manifestation of kindness from this, my once affectionate old mistress. Master Hugh was very much enraged. He gave expression to his feelings by pouring out curses upon the heads of those who did the deed. As soon as I got a little the better of my bruises, he took me with him to Esquire Watson's, on Bond Street, to see what could be done about the matter. Mr. Watson inquired who saw the assault committed. Master Hugh told him it was done in Mr. Gardner's ship-yard, at mid-day, where there were a large company of men at work. "As to that," he said, "the deed was done, and there was no question as to who did it." His answer was, he could do nothing in the case, unless some white man would come forward and testify. He could issue no warrant on my word. If I had been killed in the presence of a thousand colored people, their testimony combined would have been insufficient to have arrested one of the murderers. Master Hugh, for once, was compelled to say this state of things was too bad. Of course, it was impossible to get any white man to volunteer his testimony in my behalf, and against the white young men. Even those who may have sympathized with me were not prepared to do this. It required a degree of courage unknown to them to do so; for just at that time, the slightest manifestation of humanity toward a colored person was denounced as abolitionism, and that name subjected its bearer to frightful liabilities. The watch-words of the bloody-minded in that region, and in those days, were, "Damn the abolitionists!" and "Damn the niggers!" There was nothing done, and probably nothing would have been done if I had been killed. Such was, and such remains, the state of things in the Christian city of Baltimore.

Master Hugh, finding he could get no redress, refused to let me go back again to Mr. Gardner. He kept me himself, and his wife dressed my wound till I was again restored to health. He then took me into the ship-yard of which he was foreman, in the employment of Mr. Walter Price. There I was immediately set to calking, and very soon learned the art of using my mallet and irons. In the course of one year from the time I left Mr. Gardner's, I was able to command the highest wages given to the most experienced calkers. I was now of some importance to my master. I was bringing him from six to seven dollars per week. I sometimes brought him nine dollars per week: my wages were a dollar and a half a day. After learning how to calk, I sought my own employment, made my own contracts, and collected the money which I earned. My pathway became much more smooth than before; my condition was now much more comfortable. When I could get no calking to do, I did nothing. During these leisure times, those old notions about freedom would steal over me again. When in Mr. Gardner's employment, I was kept in such a perpetual whirl of excitement, I could think of nothing, scarcely, but my life; and in thinking of my life, I almost forgot my liberty. I have observed this in my experience of slavery,—that whenever my condition was improved, instead of its increasing my contentment, it only increased my desire to be free, and set me to thinking of plans to gain my freedom. I have found that, to make a contented slave, it is necessary to make a thoughtless one. It is necessary to darken his moral and mental vision, and, as far as possible, to annihilate the power of reason. He must be able to detect no inconsistencies in slavery; he must be made to feel that slavery is right; and he can be brought to that only when he ceases to be a man.

I was now getting, as I have said, one dollar and fifty cents per day. I contracted for it; I earned it; it was paid to me; it was rightfully my own; yet, upon each returning Saturday night, I was compelled to deliver every cent of that money to Master Hugh. And why? Not because he earned it,—not because he had any hand in earning it,—not because I owed it to him,—nor because he possessed the slightest shadow of a right to it; but solely because he had the power to compel me to give it up. The right of the grim-visaged pirate upon the high seas is exactly the same.

CHAPTER XI

I now come to that part of my life during which I planned, and finally succeeded in making, my escape from slavery. But before narrating any of the peculiar circumstances, I deem it proper to make known my intention not to state all the facts connected with the transaction. My reasons for pursuing this course may be understood from the following: First, were I to give a minute statement of all the facts, it is not only possible, but quite probable, that others would thereby be involved in the most embarrassing difficulties. Secondly, such a statement would most undoubtedly induce greater vigilance on the part of slaveholders than has existed heretofore among them; which would, of course, be the means of guarding a door whereby some dear brother bondman might escape his galling chains. I deeply regret the necessity that impels me to suppress any thing of importance connected with my experience in slavery. It would afford me great pleasure indeed, as well as materially add to the interest of my narrative, were I at liberty to gratify a curiosity, which I know exists in the minds of many, by an accurate statement of all the facts pertaining to my most fortunate escape. But I must deprive myself of this pleasure, and the curious of the gratification which such a statement would afford. I would allow myself to suffer under the greatest imputations which evil-minded men might suggest, rather than exculpate myself, and thereby run the hazard of closing the slightest avenue by which a brother slave might clear himself of the chains and fetters of slavery.

I have never approved of the very public manner in which some of our western friends have conducted what they call the *underground railroad,* but which, I think, by their open declarations, has been made most emphatically the *upperground railroad.* I honor those good men and women for their noble daring, and applaud them for willingly subjecting themselves to bloody persecution, by openly avowing their participation in the escape of slaves. I, however, can see very little good resulting from such a course, either to themselves or the slaves escaping; while, upon the other hand, I see and feel assured that those open declarations are a positive evil to the slaves remaining, who are seeking to escape. They do nothing towards enlightening the slave, whilst they do much towards enlightening the master. They stimulate him to greater watchfulness, and enhance his power to capture his slave. We owe something to the slaves south of the line as well as to those north of it; and in aiding the latter on their way to freedom, we should be careful to do nothing which would be likely to hinder the former from escaping from slavery. I would keep the merciless slaveholder profoundly ignorant of the means of flight adopted by the slave. I would leave him to imagine himself surrounded by myriads of invisible tormentors, ever ready to snatch from his infernal grasp his trembling prey. Let him be left to feel his way in the dark; let darkness commensurate with his crime hover over him; and let him feel that at every step he takes, in pursuit of the flying bondman, he is running the frightful risk of having his hot brains dashed out by an invisible agency. Let us render the tyrant no aid; let us not hold the light by which he can trace the footprints of our flying brother. But enough of this. I will now proceed to the statement of those facts, connected with my escape, for which I am alone responsible, and for which no one can be made to suffer by myself.

In the early part of the year 1838, I became quite restless. I could see no reason why I should, at the end of each week, pour the reward of my toil into the purse of my master. When I carried to him my weekly wages, he would, after counting the money, look me in the face with a robber-like fierceness, and ask, "Is this all?" He was satisfied with nothing less than the last cent. He would, however, when I made him six dollars, sometimes give me six cents, to encourage me. It had the opposite effect. I regarded it as a sort of admission of my right to the whole. The fact that he gave me any part of my wages was proof, to my mind, that he believed me entitled to the whole of them. I always felt worse for having received any thing; for I feared that the giving me a few cents would ease his conscience, and make him feel himself to be a pretty honorable sort of robber. My discontent grew upon me.

I was ever on the look-out for means of escape; and, finding no direct means, I determined to try to hire my time, with a view of getting money with which to make my escape. In the spring of 1838, when Master Thomas came to Baltimore to purchase his spring goods, I got an opportunity, and applied to him to allow me to hire my time. He unhesitatingly refused my request, and told me this was another stratagem by which to escape. He told me I could go nowhere but that he could get me; and that, in the event of my running away, he should spare no pains in his efforts to catch me. He exhorted me to content myself, and be obedient. He told me, if I would be happy, I must lay out no plans for the future. He said, if I behaved myself properly, he would take care of me. Indeed, he advised me to complete thoughtlessness of the future, and taught me to depend solely upon him for happiness. He seemed to see fully the pressing necessity of setting aside my intellectual nature, in order to contentment in slavery. But in spite of him, and even in spite of myself, I continued to think, and to think about the injustice of my enslavement, and the means of escape.

About two months after this, I applied to Master Hugh for the privilege of hiring my time. He was not acquainted with the fact that I had applied to Master Thomas, and had been refused. He too, at first, seemed disposed to refuse; but, after some reflection, he granted me the privilege, and proposed the following terms: I was to be allowed all my time, make all contracts with those for whom I worked, and find my own employment; and, in return for this liberty, I was to pay him three dollars at the end of each week; find myself in calking tools, and in board and clothing. My board was two dollars and a half per week. This, with the wear and tear of clothing and calking tools, made my regular expenses about six dollars per week. This amount I was compelled to make up, or relinquish the privilege of hiring my time. Rain or shine, work or no work, at the end of each week the money must be forthcoming, or I must give up my privilege. This arrangement, it will be perceived, was decidedly in my master's favor. It relieved him of all need of looking after me. His money was sure. He received all the benefits of slaveholding without its evils; while I endured all the evils of a slave, and suffered all the care and anxiety of a freeman. I found it a hard bargain. But, hard as it was, I thought it better than the old mode of getting along. It was a step towards freedom to be allowed to bear the responsibilities of a freeman, and I was determined to hold on upon it. I bent myself to the work of making money. I was ready to work at night as well as day, and by the most untiring perseverance and industry, I made enough to meet my expenses, and lay up a little money every week. I went on thus from May till August. Master Hugh then refused to allow me to hire my time longer. The ground for his refusal was a failure on my part, one Saturday night, to pay him for my week's time. This failure was occasioned by my attending a camp meeting about ten miles from Baltimore. During the week, I had entered into an engagement with a number of young friends to start from Baltimore to the camp ground early Saturday evening; and being detained by my employer, I was unable to get down to Master Hugh's without disappointing the company. I knew that Master Hugh was in no special need of the money that night. I therefore decided to go to the camp meeting, and upon my return pay him the three dollars. I staid at the camp meeting one day longer than I intended when I left. But as soon as I returned, I called upon him to pay him what he considered his due. I found him very angry; he could scarce restrain his wrath. He said he had a great mind to give me a severe whipping. He wished to know how I dared go out of the city without asking his permission. I told him I hired my time, and while I paid him the price which he asked for it, I did not know that I was bound to ask him when and where I should go. This reply troubled him; and, after reflecting a few moments, he turned to me, and said I should hire my time no longer; that the next thing he should know of, I would be running away. Upon the same plea, he told me to bring my tools and clothing home forthwith. I did so; but instead of seeking work, as I had been accustomed to do previously to hiring my time, I spent the whole week without the performance of a single stroke of work. I did this in retaliation. Saturday night, he called upon me as usual for my week's wages. I told him I had no wages; I had done no work that week. Here we were upon the point of coming to blows. He raved, and swore his determination to get hold of me. I did not allow myself a single word; but was resolved, if he laid the weight of his hand upon me, it should be blow for blow. He did not strike me, but told me that he would find me in constant employment in future. I thought the matter over during the next day, Sunday, and finally resolved upon the third day of September, as the day upon which I would make a second attempt to secure my freedom. I now had three weeks during which to prepare for my journey. Early on Monday morning, before Master Hugh had time to make any engagement for me, I went out and got employment of Mr. Butler, at his shipyard near the drawbridge, upon what is called the City Block, thus making it unnecessary for him to seek employment for me. At the end of the week, I brought him between eight and nine dollars. He seemed very well pleased, and asked me why I did not do the same the week before. He little knew what my plans were. My object in working steadily was to remove any suspicion he might entertain of my intent to run away; and in this I succeeded admirably. I suppose he thought I was never better satisfied with my condition than at the very time during which I was planning my escape. The second week passed, and again I carried him my full wages; and so well pleased was he, that he gave me twenty-five cents, (quite a large sum for a slaveholder to give a slave,) and bade me to make a good use of it. I told him I would.

Things went on without very smoothly indeed, but within there was trouble. It is impossible for me to describe my feelings as the time of my contemplated start drew near. I had a number of warm-hearted friends in Baltimore,—friends that I loved almost as I did my life,—and the thought of being separated from them forever was painful beyond expression. It is my opinion that thousands would escape from slavery, who now remain, but for the strong cords of affection that bind them to their friends. The thought of leaving my friends was decidedly the most painful thought with which I had to contend. The love of them was my tender point, and shook my decision more than all things else. Besides the pain of separation, the dread and apprehension of a failure exceeded what I had experienced at my first attempt. The appalling defeat I then sustained returned to torment me. I felt assured that, if I failed in this attempt, my case would be a hopeless one—it would seal my fate as a slave forever. I could not hope to get off with any thing less than the severest punishment, and being placed beyond the means of escape. It required no very vivid imagination to depict the most frightful scenes through which I should have to pass, in case I failed. The wretchedness of slavery, and the blessedness of freedom, were perpetually before me. It was life and death with me. But I remained firm, and, according to my resolution, on the third day of September, 1838, I left my chains, and succeeded in reaching New York without the slightest interruption of any kind. How I did so,—what means I adopted,—what direction I travelled, and by what mode of conveyance,—I must leave unexplained, for the reasons before mentioned.

I have been frequently asked how I felt when I found myself in a free State. I have never been able to answer the question with any satisfaction to myself. It was a moment of the highest excitement I ever experienced. I suppose I felt as one may imagine the unarmed mariner to feel when he is rescued by a friendly man-of-war from the pursuit of a pirate. In writing to a dear friend, immediately after my arrival at New York, I said I felt like one who had escaped a den of hungry lions. This state of mind, however, very soon subsided; and I was again seized with a feeling of great insecurity and loneliness. I was yet liable to be taken back, and subjected to all the tortures of slavery. This in itself was enough to damp the ardor of my enthusiasm. But the loneliness overcame me. There I was in the midst of thousands, and yet a perfect stranger; without home and without friends, in the midst of thousands of my own brethren—children of a common Father, and yet I dared not to unfold to any one of them my sad condition. I was afraid to speak to any one for fear of speaking to the wrong one, and thereby falling into the hands of money-loving kidnappers, whose business it was to lie in wait for the panting fugitive, as the ferocious beasts of the forest lie in wait for their prey. The motto which I adopted when I started from slavery was this—"Trust no man!" I saw in every white man an enemy, and in almost every colored man cause for distrust. It was a most painful situation; and, to understand it, one must needs experience it, or imagine himself in similar circumstances. Let him be a fugitive slave in a strange land—a land given up to be the hunting-ground for slaveholders—whose inhabitants are legalized kidnappers— where he is every moment subjected to the terrible liability of being seized upon by his fellow-men, as the hideous crocodile seizes upon his prey!—I say, let him place himself in my situation—without home or friends—without money or credit— wanting shelter, and no one to give it—wanting bread, and no money to buy it,—and at the same time let him feel that he is pursued by merciless men-hunters, and in total darkness as to what to do, where to go, or where to stay,—perfectly helpless both as to the means of defence and means of escape,—in the midst of plenty, yet suffering the terrible gnawings of hunger,—in the midst of houses, yet having no home,—among fellow-men, yet feeling as if in the midst of wild beasts, whose greediness to swallow up the trembling and half-famished fugitive is only equalled by that with which the monsters of the deep swallow up the helpless fish upon which they subsist,—I say, let him be placed in this most trying situation,—the situation in which I was placed,—then, and not till then, will he fully appreciate the hard-ships of, and know how to sympathize with, the toil-worn and whip-scarred fugitive slave.

Thank Heaven, I remained but a short time in this distressed situation, I was relieved from it by the humane hand of Mr. DAVID RUGGLES,* whose vigilance, kindness, and perseverance, I shall never forget. I am glad of an opportunity to express, as far as words can, the love and gratitude I bear him. Mr. Ruggles is now afflicted with blindness, and is himself in need of the same kind offices which he was once so forward in the performance of toward others. I had been in New York but a few days, when Mr. Ruggles sought me out, and very kindly took me to his boarding-house at the corner of Church and Lespenard Streets. Mr. Ruggles was then very deeply engaged in the memorable *Darg* case,* as well as attending to a number of other fugitive slaves, devising ways and means for their successful escape; and, though watched and hemmed in on almost every side, he seemed to be more than a match for his enemies.

Very soon after I went to Mr. Ruggles, he wished to know of me where I wanted to go; as he deemed it unsafe for me to remain in New York. I told him I was a calker, and should like to go where I could get work. I thought of going to Canada; but he decided against it, and in favor of my going to New Bedford, thinking I should be able to get work there at my trade. At this time, Anna,[1] my intended wife,* came on; for I wrote to her immediately after my arrival at New York, (notwithstanding my homeless, houseless, and helpless condition,) informing her of my successful flight, and wishing her to come on forthwith. In a few days after her arrival, Mr. Ruggles called in the Rev. J. W. C. Pennington,* who, in the presence of Mr. Ruggles, Mrs. Michaels, and two or three others, performed the marriage ceremony, and gave us a certificate, of which the following is an exact copy:—

"THIS may certify, that I joined together in holy matrimony Frederick Johnson[2] and Anna Murray, as man and wife, in the presence of Mr. David Ruggles and Mrs. Michaels.

"JAMES W. C. PENNINGTON.

"New York, Sept. 15, 1838."

Upon receiving this certificate, and a five-dollar bill from Mr. Ruggles, I shouldered one part of our baggage, and Anna took up the other, and we set out forthwith to take passage on board of the steamboat John W. Richmond for Newport, on our way to New Bedford. Mr. Ruggles gave me a letter to a Mr. Shaw in Newport, and told me, in case my money did not serve me to New Bedford, to stop in Newport and obtain further assistance; but upon our arrival at Newport, we were so anxious to get to a place of safety, that, notwithstanding we lacked the necessary money to pay our fare, we decided to take seats in the stage, and promise to pay when we got to New Bedford. We were encouraged to do this by two excellent gentlemen, residents of New Bedford, whose names

---

[1] She was free. [Douglass's note]

[2] I had changed my name from Frederick *Bailey* to that of Johnson. [Douglass's note]

I afterward ascertained to be Joseph Ricketson and William C. Taber. They seemed at once to understand our circumstances, and gave us such assurance of their friendliness as put us fully at ease in their presence. It was good indeed to meet with such friends, at such a time. Upon reaching New Bedford, we were directed to the house of Mr. Nathan Johnson, by whom we were kindly received, and hospitably provided for. Both Mr. and Mrs. Johnson took a deep and lively interest in our welfare. They proved themselves quite worthy of the name of abolitionists. When the stage-driver found us unable to pay our fare, he held on upon our baggage as security for the debt. I had but to mention the fact to Mr. Johnson, and he forthwith advanced the money.

We now began to feel a degree of safety, and to prepare ourselves for the duties and responsibilities of a life of freedom. On the morning after our arrival at New Bedford, while at the breakfast-table, the question arose as to what name I should be called by. The name given me by my mother was, "Frederick Augustus Washington Bailey." I, however, had dispensed with the two middle names long before I left Maryland, so that I was generally known by the name of "Frederick Bailey." I started from Baltimore bearing the name of "Stanley." When I got to New York, I again changed my name to "Frederick Johnson," and thought that would be the last change. But when I got to New Bedford, I found it necessary again to change my name. The reason of this necessity was, that there were so many Johnsons in New Bedford, it was already quite difficult to distinguish between them. I gave Mr. Johnson the privilege of choosing me a name, but told him he must not take from me the name of "Frederick." I must hold on to that, to preserve a sense of my identity. Mr. Johnson had just been reading the "Lady of the Lake," and at once suggested that my name be "Douglass."* From that time until now I have been called "Frederick Douglass;" and as I am more widely known by that name than by either of the others, I shall continue to use it as my own.

I was quite disappointed at the general appearance of things in New Bedford. The impression which I had received respecting the character and condition of the people of the north, I found to be singularly erroneous. I had very strangely supposed, while in slavery, that few of the comforts, and scarcely any of the luxuries, of life were enjoyed at the north, compared with what were enjoyed by the slaveholders of the south. I probably came to this conclusion from the fact that northern people owned no slaves. I supposed that they were about upon a level with the non-slaveholding population of the south. I knew *they* were exceedingly poor, and I had been accustomed to regard their poverty as the necessary consequence of their being non-slaveholders. I had somehow imbibed the opinion that, in the absence of slaves, there could be no wealth, and very little refinement. And upon coming to the north, I expected to meet with a rough, hard-handed, and uncultivated population, living in the most Spartan-like simplicity, knowing nothing of the ease, luxury, pomp, and grandeur of southern slaveholders. Such being my conjectures, any one acquainted with the appearance of New Bedford may very readily infer how palpably I must have seen my mistake.

In the afternoon of the day when I reached New Bedford, I visited the wharves, to take a view of the shipping. Here I found myself surrounded with the strongest proofs of wealth. Lying at the wharves, and riding in the stream, I saw many ships of the finest models, in the best order, and of the largest size. Upon the right and left, I was walled in by granite warehouses of the widest dimensions, stowed to their utmost capacity with the necessaries and comforts of life. Added to this, almost every body seemed to be at work, but noiselessly so, compared with what I had been accustomed to in Baltimore. There were no loud songs heard from those engaged in loading and unloading ships. I heard no deep oaths or horrid curses on the laborer. I saw no whipping of men; but all seemed to go smoothly on. Every man appeared to understand his work, and went at it with a sober, yet cheerful earnestness, which betokened the deep interest which he felt in what he was doing, as well as a sense of his own dignity as a man. To me this looked exceedingly strange. From the wharves I strolled around and over the town, gazing with wonder and admiration at the splendid churches, beautiful dwellings, and finely-cultivated gardens; evincing an amount of wealth, comfort, taste, and refinement, such as I had never seen in any part of slaveholding Maryland.

Every thing looked clean, new, and beautiful. I saw few or no dilapidated houses, with poverty-stricken inmates; no half-naked children and barefooted women, such as I had been accustomed to see in Hillsborough, Easton, St. Michael's, and Baltimore. The people looked more able, stronger, healthier, and happier, than those of Maryland. I was for once made glad by a view of extreme wealth, without being saddened by seeing extreme poverty. But the most astonishing as well as the most interesting thing to me was the condition of the colored people, a great many of whom, like myself, had escaped thither as a refuge from the hunters of men. I found many, who had not been seven years out of their chains, living in finer houses, and evidently enjoying more of the comforts of life, than the average of slaveholders in Maryland. I will venture to assert that my friend Mr. Nathan Johnson (of whom I can say with a grateful heart, "I was hungry, and he gave me meat; I was thirsty, and he gave me drink; I was a stranger, and he took me in")* lived in a neater house; dined at a better table; took, paid for, and read, more newspapers; better understood the moral, religious, and political character of the nation,—than nine tenths of the slaveholders in Talbot county, Maryland. Yet Mr. Johnson was a working man. His hands were hardened by toil, and not his alone, but those also of Mrs. Johnson. I found the colored people much more spirited than I had supposed they would be. I found among them a determination to protect each other from the blood-thirsty kidnapper, at all hazards. Soon after my arrival, I was told of a circumstance which illustrated their spirit. A colored man and a fugitive slave were on unfriendly terms. The former was heard to threaten the latter with informing his master of his whereabouts. Straightway a meeting was called among the colored people, under the stereotyped notice, "Business of importance!" The betrayer was invited to attend. The people came at the appointed hour, and organized the meeting by appointing a very religious old gentleman as president, who, I believe, made a prayer, after which he addressed the meeting as follows: *"Friends, we have got him here, and I would recom-*

mend that you young men just take him outside the door, and kill him!" With this, a number of them bolted at him; but they were intercepted by some more timid than themselves, and the betrayer escaped their vengeance, and has not been seen in New Bedford since. I believe there have been no more such threats, and should there be hereafter, I doubt not that death would be the consequence.

I found employment, the third day after my arrival, in stowing a sloop with a load of oil. It was new, dirty, and hard work for me; but I went at it with a glad heart and a willing hand. I was now my own master. It was a happy moment, the rapture of which can be understood only by those who have been slaves. It was the first work, the reward of which was to be entirely my own. There was no Master Hugh standing ready, the moment I earned the money, to rob me of it. I worked that day with a pleasure I had never before experienced. I was at work for myself and newly-married wife. It was to me the starting-point of a new existence. When I got through with that job, I went in pursuit of a job of calking; but such was the strength of prejudice against color, among the white calkers, that they refused to work with me, and of course I could get no employment.[1] Finding my trade of no immediate benefit, I threw off my calking habiliments, and prepared myself to do any kind of work I could get to do. Mr. Johnson kindly let me have his wood-horse and saw, and I very soon found myself a plenty of work. There was no work too hard—none too dirty. I was ready to saw wood, shovel coal, carry the hod,* sweep the chimney, or roll oil casks,—all of which I did for nearly three years in New Bedford, before I became known to the anti-slavery world.

In about four months after I went to New Bedford, there came a young man to me, and inquired if I did not wish to take the "Liberator." I told him I did; but, just having made my escape from slavery, I remarked that I was unable to pay for it then. I, however, finally became a subscriber to it. The paper came, and I read it from week to week with such feelings as it would be quite

---

[1] I am told that colored persons can now get employment at calking in New Bedford—a result of anti-slavery effort. [Douglass's note]

idle for me to attempt to describe. The paper became my meat and my drink. My soul was set all on fire. Its sympathy for my brethren in bonds—its scathing denunciations of slaveholders—its faithful exposures of slavery—and its powerful attacks upon the upholders of the institution—sent a thrill of joy through my soul, such as I had never felt before!

I had not long been a reader of the "Liberator," before I got a pretty correct idea of the principles, measures and spirit of the anti-slavery reform. I took right hold of the cause. I could do but little; but what I could, I did with a joyful heart, and never felt happier than when in an anti-slavery meeting. I seldom had much to say at the meetings, because what I wanted to say was said so much better by others. But, while attending an anti-slavery convention at Nantucket, on the 11th of August, 1841, I felt strongly moved to speak, and was at the same time much urged to do so by Mr. William C. Coffin, a gentleman who had heard me speak in the colored people's meeting at New Bedford. It was a severe cross, and I took it up reluctantly. The truth was, I felt myself a slave, and the idea of speaking to white people weighed me down. I spoke but a few moments, when I felt a degree of freedom, and said what I desired with considerable ease. From that time until now, I have been engaged in pleading the cause of my brethren—with what success, and with what devotion, I leave those acquainted with my labors to decide.

APPENDIX

I find, since reading over the foregoing Narrative, that I have, in several instances, spoken in such a tone and manner, respecting religion, as may possibly lead those unacquainted with my religious views to suppose me an opponent of all religion. To remove the liability of such misapprehension, I deem it proper to append the following brief explanation. What I have said respecting and against religion, I mean strictly to apply to the *slaveholding religion* of this land, and with no possible reference to Christianity proper; for, between the Christianity of this land, and the Christianity of Christ, I recognize the widest possible difference—so wide, that to receive the one as good, pure, and holy, is of necessity to reject the other as bad, corrupt, and wicked. To be the friend of the one, is of necessity to be the enemy of the other. I love the pure, peaceable, and impartial Christianity of Christ: I therefore hate the corrupt, slaveholding, women-whipping, cradle-plundering, partial and hypocritical Christianity of this land. Indeed, I can see no reason, but the most deceitful one, for calling the religion of this land Christianity. I look upon it as the climax of all misnomers, the boldest of all frauds, and the grossest of all libels. Never was there a clearer case of "stealing the livery of the court of heaven to serve the devil in."* I am filled with unutterable loathing when I contemplate the religious pomp and show, together with the horrible inconsistencies, which every where surround me. We have men-stealers for ministers, women-whippers for missionaries, and cradle-plunderers for church members. The man who wields the blood-clotted cowskin during the week fills the pulpit on Sunday, and claims to be a minister of the meek and lowly Jesus. The man who robs me of my earnings at the end of each week meets me as a class-leader on Sunday morning, to show me the way of life, and the path of salvation. He who sells my sister, for purposes of prostitution, stands forth as the pious advocate of purity. He who proclaims it a religious duty to read the Bible denies me the right of learning to read the name of the God who made me. He who is the religious advocate of marriage robs whole millions of its sacred influence, and leaves them to the ravages of wholesale pollution. The warm defender of the sacredness of the family relation is the same that scatters whole families,—sundering husbands and wives, parents and children, sisters and brothers,—leaving the hut vacant, and the hearth desolate. We see the thief preaching against theft, and the adulterer against adultery. We have men sold to build churches, women sold to support the gospel, and babes sold to purchase Bibles for the *poor heathen! all for the glory of God and the good of soul!* The slave auctioneer's bell and the church-going bell chime in with each other, and the bitter cries of the heart-broken slave are drowned in the religious shouts of his pious master. Revivals of religion and revivals in the slave-trade go hand in hand together. The slave prison and the church stand near each other. The clanking of fetters and the rattling of chains in the prison, and the pious psalm and solemn prayer in the church, may be heard at the same time. The dealers in the bodies and souls of men erect their stand in the presence of the pulpit, and they mutually help each other. The dealer gives his blood-stained gold to support the pulpit, and the pulpit, in return, covers his infernal business with the garb of Christianity. Here we have religion and robbery the allies of each other—devils dressed in angels' robes, and hell presenting the semblance of paradise.

> "Just God! and these are they,
>   Who minister at thine altar, God of right!
> Men who their hands, with prayer and blessing, lay
>   On Israel's ark of light.*
>
> "What! preach, and kidnap men?
>   Give thanks, and rob thy own afflicted poor?
> Talk of thy glorious liberty, and then
>   Bolt hard the captive's door?
>
> "What! servants of thy own
>   Merciful Son, who came to seek and save
> The homeless and the outcast, fettering down
>   The tasked and plundered slave!

"Pilate and Herod friends!*
Chief priests and rulers, as of old, combine!
Just God and holy! is that church which lends
Strength to the spoiler thine?"*

The Christianity of America is a Christianity, of whose votaries it may be as truly said, as it was of the ancient scribes and Pharisees,* "They bind heavy burdens, and grievous to be borne, and lay them on men's shoulders, but they themselves will not move them with one of their fingers. All their works they do for to be seen of men. —— They love the uppermost rooms at feasts, and the chief seats in the synagogues, . . . and to be called of men, Rabbi, Rabbi. —— But woe unto you, scribes and Pharisees, hypocrites! for ye shut up the kingdom of heaven against men; for ye neither go in yourselves, neither suffer ye them that are entering to go in. Ye devour widows' houses, and for a pretence make long prayers; therefore ye shall receive the greater damnation. Ye compass sea and land to make one proselyte, and when he is made, ye make him twofold more the child of hell than yourselves. —— Woe unto you, scribes and Pharisees, hypocrites! for ye pay tithe of mint, and anise, and cumin, and have omitted the weightier matters of the law, judgment, mercy, and faith; these ought ye to have done, and not to leave the other undone. Ye blind guides! which strain at a gnat, and swallow a camel. Woe unto you, scribes and Pharisees, hypocrites! for ye make clean the outside of the cup of the platter; but within, they are full of extortion and excess. —— Woe unto you, scribes and Pharisees, hypocrites! for ye are like unto whited sepulchres, which indeed appear beautiful outward, but are within full of dead men's bones, and of all uncleanness. Even so ye also outwardly appear righteous unto men, but within ye are full of hypocrisy and iniquity."

Dark and terrible as is this picture, I hold it to be strictly true of the overwhelming mass of professed Christians in America. They strain at a gnat, and swallow a camel. Could any thing be more true of our churches? They would be shocked at the proposition of fellowshipping a *sheep*-stealer; and at the same time they hug to their communion a *man*-stealer, and brand me with being an infidel, if I find fault with them for it. They attend with

Pharisaical strictness to the outward forms of religion, and at the same time neglect the weightier matters of the law, judgment, mercy, and faith. They are always ready to sacrifice, but seldom to show mercy. They are they who are represented as professing to love God whom they have not seen, whilst they hate their brother whom they have seen. They love the heathen on the other side of the globe. They can pray for him, pay money to have the Bible put into his hand, and missionaries to instruct him; while they despise and totally neglect the heathen at their own doors.

Such is, very briefly, my view of the religion of this land; and to avoid any misunderstanding, growing out of the use of general terms, I mean, by the religion of this land, that which is revealed in the words, deeds, and actions, of those bodies, north and south, calling themselves Christian churches, and yet in union with slaveholders. It is against religion, as presented by these bodies, that I have felt it my duty to testify.

I conclude these remarks by copying the following portrait of the religion of the south, (which is, by communion and fellowship, the religion of the north,) which I soberly affirm is "true to the life," and without caricature or the slightest exaggeration. It is said to have been drawn, several years before the present anti-slavery agitation began, by a northern Methodist preacher, who, while residing at the south, had an opportunity to see slaveholding morals, manners, and piety, with his own eyes. "Shall I not visit for these things? saith the Lord. Shall not my soul be avenged on such a nation as this?"*

A PARODY*

"Come, saints and sinners, hear me tell
How pious priests whip Jack and Nell,
And women buy and children sell,
And preach all sinners down to hell,
    And sing of heavenly union.

"They'll beat and baa, dona like goats,
Gorge down black sheep, and strain at motes,
Array their backs in fine black coats,

Then seize their negroes by their throats,
 And choke, for heavenly union.

"They'll church you if you sip a dram,
And damn you if you steal a lamb;
Yet rob old Tony, Doll, and Sam,
Of human rights, and bread and ham;
 Kidnapper's heavenly union.

"They'll loudly talk of Christ's reward,
And bind his image with a cord,
And scold, and wing the lash abhorred,
And sell their brother in the Lord
 To handcuffed heavenly union.

"They'll read and sing a sacred song,
And make a prayer both loud and long,
And teach the right and do the wrong,
Hailing the brother, sister throng,
 With words of heavenly union.

"We wonder how such saints can sing,
Or praise the Lord upon the wing,
Who roar, and scold, and whip, and sting,
And to their slaves and mammon cling,
 In guilty conscience union.

"They'll raise tobacco, corn, and rye,
And drive, and thieve, and cheat, and lie,
And lay up treasures in the sky,
By making switch and cowskin fly,
 In hope of heavenly union.

"They'll crack old Tony on the skull,
And preach and roar like Bashan bull,*
Or braying ass, of mischief full,
Then seize old Jacob by the wool,
 And pull for heavenly union.

"A roaring, ranting, sleek man-thief,
Who lived on mutton, veal, and beef,
Yet never would afford relief
To needy, sable sons of grief,
 Was big with heavenly union.

" 'Love not the world,' the preacher said,
And winked his eye, and shook his head;
He seized on Tom, and Dick, and Ned,
Cut short their meat, and clothes, and bread,
    Yet still loved heavenly union.

"Another preacher whining spoke
Of One whose heart for sinners broke:
He tied old Nanny to an oak,
And drew the blood at every stroke,
    And prayed for heavenly union.

"Two others oped their iron jaws,
And waved their children-stealing paws;
There sat their children in gewgaws;
By stinting negroes' backs and maws,
    They kept up heavenly union.

"All good from Jack another takes,
And entertains their flirts and rakes,
Who dress as sleek as glossy snakes,
And cram their mouths with sweetened cakes;
    And this goes down for union."

Sincerely and earnestly hoping that this little book may do something toward throwing light on the American slave system, and hastening the glad day of deliverance to the millions of my brethren in bonds—faithfully relying upon the power of truth, love, and justice, for success in my humble efforts—and solemnly pledging myself anew to the sacred cause,—I subscribe myself,

                                   FREDERICK DOUGLASS

Lynn, *Mass., April 28,* 1845

APPENDIX I

The Testimony of Angelina Grimké Weld

In 1839 the American Anti-Slavery Society published *American Slavery As It Is*, a compilation of first-hand accounts of the horrors of slavery. A hugely influential abolitionist tract, it was used by Douglass as well as Harriet Beecher Stowe in *Uncle Tom's Cabin*. The following testimony is by Angelina Grimké Weld, described as 'the youngest daughter of the late Judge Grimké, of the Supreme Court of South Carolina, and a sister of the late Hon. Thomas S. Grimké, of Charleston'.

FORT LEE, BERGEN CO., NEW JERSEY,
Fourth month 6th, 1839

I sit down to comply with thy request, preferred in the name of the Executive Committee of the American Anti-Slavery Society. The responsibility laid upon me by such a request, leaves me no option. While I live, and slavery lives, I *must* testify against it. If I should hold my peace, "the stone would cry out of the wall, and the beam out of the timber would answer it." But though I feel a necessity upon me, and "a woe unto me," if I withhold my testimony, I give it with a heavy heart. My flesh crieth out, "if it be possible, let *this* cup pass from me;" but, "Father, *thy* will be done," is, I trust, the breathing of my spirit. Oh, the slain of the daughter of my people! They lie in all the ways; their tears fall as the rain, and are their meat day and night; their blood runneth down like water; their plundered hearths are desolate; they weep for their husbands and children, because they are not; and the proud waves do continually go over them, while no eye pitieth, and no man careth for their souls.

But it is not alone for the sake of my poor brothers and sisters in bonds, or for the cause of truth, and righteousness, and humanity, that I testify; the deep yearnings of affection for the mother that bore me, who is still a slaveholder, both in fact and in heart; for my brothers and sisters, (a large family circle,) and for my numerous other slaveholding kindred in South Carolina, constrain me to speak:

for even were slavery no curse to its victims, the exercise of arbitrary power works such fearful ruin upon the hearts of *slaveholders,* that I should feel impelled to labor and pray for its overthrow with my last energies and latest breath.

I think it important to premise, that I have seen almost nothing of slavery on *plantations.* My testimony will have respect exclusively to the treatment of *"house-servants,"* and chiefly those belonging to the first families in the city of Charleston, both in the religious and in the fashionable world. And here let me say, that the treatment of *plantation* slaves cannot be fully known, except by the poor sufferers themselves, and their drivers and overseers. In a multitude of instances, even the master can know very little of the actual condition of his own field slaves, and his wife and daughters far less. A few facts concerning my own family will show this. Our permanent residence was in Charleston; our country-seat (Bellemont,) was 200 miles distant, in the northwestern part of the state; where, for some years, our family spent a few months annually. Our *plantation* was three miles from this family mansion. There, all the field slaves lived and worked. Occasionally, once a month, perhaps, some of the family would ride over to the plantation, but I never visited the *fields where the slaves were at work,* and knew almost nothing of their condition; but this I do know, that the overseers who had charge of them, were generally unprincipled and intemperate men. But I rejoice to know, that the general treatment of slaves in that region of country, was far milder than on the plantations in the lower country.

Throughout all the eastern and middle portions of the state, the planters very rarely reside permanently on their plantations. They have almost invariably *two* residences, and spend less than half the year on their estates. Even while spending a few months on them, politics, field sports, races, speculations, journeys, visits, company, literary pursuits, &c., absorb so much of their time, that they must, to a considerable extent, take the condition of their slaves on *trust,* from the reports of their overseers. I make this statement, because these slaveholders (the wealthier class,) are, I believe, almost the only ones who visit the north with their families;—and northern opinions of slavery are based chiefly on their testimony.

But not to dwell on preliminaries. I wish to record my testimony to the faithfulness and accuracy with which my beloved sister, Sarah M. Grimké, has, in her "narrative and testimony," on a preceding page described the condition of the slaves, and the effect upon the hearts of slaveholders, (even the best,) caused by the exercise of unlimited power over moral agents. Of the *particular* acts which she has stated, I have no personal knowledge, as they occurred before my remembrance; but of the spirit that prompted them, and that constantly displays itself in scenes of similar horror, the recollections of my childhood, and the effaceless imprint upon my riper years, with the breaking of my heartstrings, when, finding that I was powerless to shield the victims, I tore myself from my home and friends, and became an exile among strangers—all these throng around me as witnesses, and their testimony is graven on my memory with a pen of fire.

Why I did not become totally hardened, under the daily operation of this system, God only knows; in deep solemnity and gratitude. I say, it was the *Lord's* doing, and marvellous in mine eyes. Even before my heart was touched with the love of Christ, I used to say, "Oh that I had the wings of a dove, that I might flee away and be at rest;" for I felt that there could be no rest for me in the midst of such outrages and pollutions. And yet I saw *nothing* of slavery in its most vulgar and repulsive forms. I saw it in the *city*, among the fashionable and the honorable, where it was garnished by refinement, and decked out for show. A few *facts* will unfold the state of society in the circle with which I was familiar, far better than any general assertions I can make.

I will first introduce the reader to a woman of the highest respectability—one who was foremost in every benevolent enterprise, and stood for many years, I may say, at the *head* of the fashionable élite of the city of Charleston, and afterwards at the head of the moral and religious female society there. It was after she had made a profession of religion, and retired from the fashionable world, that I knew her; therefore I will present her in her religious character. This lady used to keep cowhides, or small paddles, (called "pancake sticks,") in four different apartments in her house; so that when she wished to punish, or to have punished, any of her slaves, she might not have the trouble of sending for an instrument of torture. For many years, one or other, and *often* more of her slaves, were flogged *every day;* particularly the young slaves about the house; whose faces were slapped, or their hands beat with the "pancake stick," for every trifling offence—and often for no fault at all. But the floggings were not all; the scoldings and abuse daily heaped upon them all, were worse: "fools" and "liars" "sluts" and "husseys," "hypocrites" and "good-for-nothing creatures," were the *common* epithets with which her mouth was filled, when addressing her slaves, adults as well as children. Very often she would take a position at her window, in an upper story, and scold at her slaves while working in the garden, at some distance from the house, (a large yard intervening,) and occasionally order a flogging. I have known her thus on the watch, scolding for more than an hour at a time, in so loud a voice that the whole neighborhood could hear her, and this without the least apparent feeling of shame. Indeed, it was *no disgrace among slave-holders,* and did not in the least injure her standing, either as a lady or a Christian, in the aristocratic circle in which she moved. After the "revival" in Charleston, in 1825, she opened her house to social prayer-meetings. The room in which they were held in the evening, and where the voice of prayer was heard around the family altar, and where she herself retired for private devotion thrice each day, was the very place in which, when her slaves were to be whipped with the cowhide, they were taken to receive the infliction; and the wail of the sufferer would be heard, where, perhaps only a few hours previous, rose voices of prayer and praise. This mistress would occasionally send her slaves, male and female, to the Charleston work-house to be punished. One poor girl, whom she sent there to be flogged, and who was accordingly stripped *naked* and whipped, showed me the deep gashes on her back—I might have laid my whole finger in them—*large pieces of flesh had actually been cut out by the torturing lash.* She sent another female slave there, to be imprisoned and worked on the treadmill. This girl was confined several days, and forced to work the mill while in a state of suffering from another cause. For ten days or two weeks after her return, she was lame, from the violent exertion necessary to enable her to keep the step on the machine. She spoke to me with intense feeling of this outrage upon her, as a *woman.* Her men servants were sometimes flogged there; and so exceedingly offensive has been the putrid flesh of their lacerated backs, for days after the infliction, that they would be kept out of the house—the smell arising from their wounds being too horrible to be endured. They were always stiff and sore for some days, and not in a condition to be seen by visitors.

This professedly Christian woman was a most awful illustration of the ruinous influence of arbitrary power upon the temper—her bursts of passion upon the heads of her victims were dreaded even by her own children, and very often, all the pleasure of social inter-course around the domestic board, was destroyed by her ordering the cook into her presence, and storming at him, when the dinner or breakfast was not prepared to her taste, and in the presence of all her children, commanding the waiter to slap his face. *Fault-finding*, was with her the constant accompaniment of every meal, and banished that peace which should hover around the social board, and smile on every face. It was common for her to order brothers to whip their own sisters, and sisters their own brothers, and yet no woman visited among the poor more than she did; or gave more liberally to relieve their wants. This may seem perfectly unaccountable to a northerner, but these seeming contradictions vanish when we consider that over *them* she possessed no arbitrary power, they were always presented to her mind as unfortunate sufferers, towards whom her sympathies most freely flowed; she was ever ready to wipe the tears from *their* eyes and open wide her purse for *their* relief, but the others were her *vassals*, thrust down by public opinion beneath her feet, to be at her beck and call, ever ready to serve in all humility, her, whom God in his providence had set over them—it was their *duty* to abide in abject submission, and hers to *compel* them to do so—it *was thus that she reasoned*. Except at family prayers, none were permitted to *sit* in her presence, but the seamstresses and waiting maids, and they, however delicate might be their circumstances, were forced to sit upon low stools, without backs, that they might be constantly reminded of their inferiority. A slave who waited in the house, was guilty on a particular occasion of going to visit his wife, and kept dinner waiting a little, (his wife was the slave of a lady who lived at a little distance.) When the family sat down to the table, the mistress began to scold the waiter for the offence—he attempted to excuse himself—she ordered him to hold his tongue—he ventured another apology; her son then rose from the table in a rage, and beat the face and ears of the waiter so dreadfully that the blood gushed from his mouth, and nose, and ears. This mistress was a *professor of religion;* her daughter who related the circumstance, was a *fellow member* of the Presbyterian church *with the poor outraged slave*—instead of feeling indignation at this outrageous abuse of her brother in the church, she justified the deed, and said "he got just what he deserved." I solemnly believe this to be a true picture of *slaveholding religion.*

The following circumstance occurred in Charleston, in 1828:

A slaveholder, after flogging a little girl about thirteen years old, set her on a table with her feet fastened in a pair of stocks. He then locked the door and took out the key. When the door was opened she was found dead, from having fallen from the table. When I asked a prominent lawyer, who belonged to one of the first families in the State, whether the murderer of this helpless child could not be indicted, he cooly replied, that the slave was Mr. ——'s property, and if he chose to suffer the *loss*, no one else had anything to do with it. The loss of *human life*, the distress of the parents and other relatives of the little girl, seemed utterly out of his thoughts: it was the loss of *property* only that presented itself to his mind.

I also know that an aged slave of his, (by marriage,) was allowed to get a scanty and precarious subsistence, by begging in the streets of Charleston—he was too old to work and therefore *his allowance was stopped*, and he was turned out to make his living by begging.

When I was about thirteen years old, I attended a seminary, in Charleston, which was superintended by a man and his wife of superior education. They had under their instruction the daughters of nearly all the aristocracy. Their cruelty to their slaves, both male and female, I can never forget. I remember one day there was called into the school room to open a window, a boy whose head had been shaved in order to disgrace him, and he had been so dreadfully whipped that he could hardly walk. So horrible was the impression produced upon my mind by his heart-broken countenance and crippled person that I fainted away. The sad and ghastly countenance of one of their female mulatto slaves who used to sit on a low stool at her sewing in the piazza, is now fresh before me. She often told me, secretly, how cruelly she was whipped when they sent her to the work house. I had known so much of the terrible scourgings inflicted in that house of blood, that when I was once obliged to pass it, the very sight smote me with such horror that my limbs could hardly sustain me. I felt as if I was passing the precincts of hell. A friend of mine who lived in the neighborhood, told me she often heard the screams of the slaves under their torture.

Southern mistresses sometimes flog their slaves themselves, though generally one slave is compelled to flog another. Whilst staying at a friend's house some years ago, I one day saw the mistress with a cow-hide in her hand, and heard her scolding in an undertone, her waiting man, who was about twenty-five years old. Whether she actually inflicted the blows I do not know, for I hastened out of sight and hearing. It was not the first time I had seen a mistress thus engaged. I knew she was a cruel mistress, and had heard her daughters disputing, whether their mother did right or wrong, to send the slave *children*, (whom she sent out to sweep chimneys) to the work-house to be whipped if they did not bring in their wages regularly. This woman moved in the most fashionable circle in Charleston. The income of this family was derived mostly from the hire of their slaves, about one hundred in number. Their luxuries were blood-bought luxuries indeed. And yet what stranger would ever have inferred their cruelties from the courteous reception and bland manners of the parlor. Everything cruel and revolting is carefully concealed from strangers, especially those from the north. Take an instance. I have known the master and mistress of a family send to their friends to *borrow* servants to wait on company, because their own slaves had been so cruelly flogged in the work house, that they could not walk without limping at every step, and their putrified flesh emitted such an intolerable smell that they were not fit to be in the presence of company. How can northerners know these things when they are hospitably received at southern tables and firesides? I repeat it, no one who has not be an *integral part* of a slaveholding community, can have any idea of its abominations. . . .

The utter disregard of the comfort of the slaves, in *little* things, can scarcely be conceived by those who have not been a *component part* of slaveholding communities. Take a few particulars out of hundreds that might be named. In South Carolina mosquitos swarm in myriads, more than half the year—they are so excessively annoying at night, that no family thinks of sleeping without nets of "mosquito bars" hung over their bedsteads, yet slaves are never provided with them, unless it be the favorite old domestics who get the cast-off pavilions; and yet these very masters and mistresses will be so kind to their *horses* as to provide them with *fly nets*. Bedsteads and bedding too, are rarely provided for any of the slaves—if the waiters and coachmen, waiting maids, cooks, washers, &c., have beds at all, they must generally get them for themselves. Commonly they lie down at night on the bare floor, with a small blanket wrapped round them in winter, and in summer a coarse osnaburg sheet, or nothing. Old slaves generally have beds, but it is because when younger *they have provided them for themselves.*

Only two meals a day are allowed the house slaves—the *first at twelve* o'clock. If they eat before this time, it is by stealth, and I am sure there must be a good deal of suffering among them from *hunger*, and particularly by children. Besides this, they are often kept from their meals by way of punishment. No table is provided for them to eat from. They know nothing of the comfort and pleasure of gathering round the social board—each takes his plate or tin pan and iron spoon and holds it in the hand or on the lap. I *never* saw slaves seated round a *table* to partake of any meal.

As the general rule, no lights of any kind, no firewood—no towels, basins, or soap, no tables, chairs, or other furniture, are provided. Wood for cooking and washing *for the family* is found, but when the master's work is done, the slave must find wood for himself if he has a fire. I have repeatedly known slave children kept the whole winter's evening, sitting on the staircase in a cold entry, just to be at hand to snuff candles or hand a tumbler of water from the sideboard, or go on errands from one room to another. It may be asked why they were not permitted to stay in the parlor, when they would be still more at hand. I answer, because waiters are not allowed to *sit* in the presence of their owners, and as children who were kept running all day, would of course get very tired of standing for two or three hours, they were allowed to go into the entry and sit on the staircase until rung for. Another reason is, that even slaveholders at times find the presence of slaves very annoying: they cannot exercise entire freedom of speech before them on all subjects.

Chambermaids and seamstresses often slept in their mistresses' apartments, but with no bedding at all. I know an instance of a woman who has been married eleven years, and yet has never been allowed to sleep out of her mistress's chamber.—This is a *great* hardship to slaves. When we consider that house slaves are rarely allowed social intercourse during *the day*, as their work generally *separates* them: the barbarity of such an arrangement is obvious. It is peculiarly a hardship in the above case, as the husband of the woman does not "belong" to her "owner:" and because he is subject to dreadful attacks of illness, and can have but little attention from his wife in the *day*. And yet her mistress, who is an old lady, gives her the highest character as a faithful servant, and told a friend of mine, that she was "entirely dependent upon her for *all* her comforts: she dressed and undressed her, gave her all her food, and was so *necessary* to her that she could not do without her." I may add, that this couple are tenderly attached to each other.

I also know an instance in which the husband was a slave and the wife was free: during the illness of the former, the latter was *allowed* to come and nurse him: she was obliged to leave the work by which she had made a living, and come to stay with her husband, and thus lost weeks of her time, or he would have suffered for want of proper attention: and yet his "owner" made her no compensation for her services. He had long been a faithful and favorite slave, and his owner was a woman very benevolent to the poor whites.—She went a great deal among these, as a visiting commissioner of the Ladies' Benevolent Society, and was in the constant habit of *paying the relatives of the poor whites* for nursing *their* husbands, fathers, and other relations: because she thought it very hard, when their time was taken up, so that they could not earn their daily bread, that they should be left to suffer. Now, such is the stupifying influences of the "*chattel* principle" on the minds of slaveholders, that I do not suppose it ever occurred to her that this poor *colored* wife ought to be paid for her services, and particularly as she was spending her time and strength in taking care of *her "property."* She no doubt only thought how kind she was, to *allow* her to come and stay so long in her yard: for, let it be kept in mind, that slaveholders have unlimited power to separate husbands and wives, parents and children, however and whenever they please; and if this mistress had chosen to do it, she could have debarred this woman from all intercourse with her husband, by forbidding her to enter her premises.

Persons who own plantations and yet live in cities, often take children from their parents as soon as they are weaned, and send them into the country; because they do not want the time of the mother taken up by attendance upon her own children, it being too valuable to the mistress. As a *favor*, she is, in some cases, permitted to go to see them once a year. So, on the other hand, if field slaves happen to have children of an age suitable to the convenience of the master, they are taken from their parents and brought to the city. Parents are almost never consulted as to the disposition to be made of their children: they have as little control over them, as have domestic animals over the disposal of their young. Every natural and social feeling and affection are violated with indifference; slaves are treated as though they did not possess them.

Another way in which the feelings of slaves are trifled with and often deeply wounded, is by changing their names; if, at the time they are brought into a family, there is another slave of the same name; or if the owner happens, for some other reason, not to like the name of the newcomer. I have known slaves very much grieved at having the names of their children thus changed, when they had been called after a dear relation. Indeed it would be utterly impossible to recount the multitude of ways in which the *heart* of the slave is continually lacerated by the total disregard of his feelings as a social being and a human creature.

The slave suffers also greatly from being continually *watched*. The system of espionage which is constantly kept up over slaves is the most worrying and intolerable that can be imagined. Many mistresses are, in fact, during the absence of their husbands, really their drivers; and the pleasure of returning to their families often, on the part of the husband, is entirely destroyed by the complaints preferred against the slaves when he comes home to his meals.

A mistress of my acquaintance asked her servant boy, one day, what was the reason she could not get him to do his work whilst his master was away, and said to him, "Your master works a great deal harder than you do; he is at his office all day, and often has to study his law cases at night." "Master," said the boy, "is working for himself, and for you, ma'am, but I am working for *him*." The mistress turned and remarked to a friend, that she was so struck with the truth of the remark, that she could not say a word to him.

But I forbear—the sufferings of the slaves are not only innumerable, but they are *indescribable*. I may paint the agony of kindred torn from each other's arms, to meet no more in time; I may depict the inflictions of the blood-stained lash, but I *cannot describe* the daily, hourly, ceaseless torture, endured by the heart that is constantly trampled under foot of despotic power. This is a part of the horrors of slavery which, I believe, no one has ever attempted to delineate; I wonder not at it, it mocks all power of language. Who can describe the anguish of that mind which feels itself impaled upon the iron of arbitrary power—its living, writhing, helpless victim! Every human susceptibility tortured, its sympathies torn, and stung, and bleeding—always feeling the death-weapon in its heart, and yet not so deep as to *kill* that humanity which is made the curse of its existence.

In the course of my testimony I have entered somewhat into the *minutiae* of slavery, because this is a part of the subject often overlooked, and cannot be appreciated by any but those who have been witnesses, and entered into sympathy with the slaves as human beings. Slaveholders think nothing of them, because they regard their slaves as *property*, the mere instruments of their convenience and pleasure. *One who is a slaveholder at heart never recognises a human being in a slave.*

As thou hast asked me to testify respecting the *physical condition* of the slaves merely, I say nothing of the awful neglect of their *minds* and *souls* and the systematic effort to imbrute them. A wrong and an impiety, in comparison with which all the other unutterable wrongs of slavery are but as the dust of the balance.

ANGELINA G. WELD

APPENDIX II

Selections on Women's Rights from *Frederick Douglass' Paper*

The following three articles from *Frederick Douglass' Paper* are examples of Douglass's powerful voice on behalf of women's rights and female suffrage.

Some Thoughts on Woman's Rights

Woman has been the subject most prominent in the public discussions of our city during the past week, beginning with the meetings of the "Women's New York State Temperance Society" on Wednesday morning, and ending in Corinthian Hall on Sunday evening, when a large audience were addressed by Mr. William H. Channing, and Miss Lucy Stone. The wrongs, hardships, and inequalities, moral, mental, social, civil, and political, endured by woman, were forcibly and eloquently brought forward, and doubtless made a deep impression. No man could listen to Miss Stone's address on Sunday evening, without feeling that there was much reason in her speech, and in no part of it more than in that she portrayed the perfect dearth of motive and object afforded by society to young ladies. It was shown that on leaving school, about the most which is expected of a young lady, is that she will go home and "do little pretty things to wear"—nothing more.

This is all wrong; a woman should have every honorable motive to exertion which is enjoyed by man, to the full extent of her capacities and endowments. The case is too plain for argument. Nature has given woman the same powers, and subjected her to the same earth, breathes the same air, subsists on the same food, physical, moral, mental and spiritual. She has, therefore, an equal right with man, in all efforts to obtain and maintain a perfect existence. Speaking on this subject, and the demand which woman makes upon her brothers at this time, we cannot do better than quote from *The Una*, for June, which has just come to hand. The editor says, (speaking of woman:)

"With her life all smothered on one side, it was but natural that it should be exaggerated on the other; and it was just as natural she should be compensated for being cruelly overruled, by being foolishly over-praised.—Women are not better, judged by a just and generous standard, than men. If the virgin was a woman, her divine son was a man.—This more than justice, habitually accorded to her moral nature, is but the cover for that greatly less than justice, which she has suffered in judgment and treatment at the hands of men. We ask for her less flattery, less adulation and more equity, fewer compliments and more completeness—fewer fair words and more fair treatment. We ask equal opportunity for free development, equal access to advantageous positions, equal wages for equal work, and equal rights for equal capacities. We cannot live upon incense, and he would not live upon alms. We are unwilling to be worshipped, for well we know that in the world's religion it means turning us out of the earth, under pretense of sending us to heaven. We are the abolitionists of slavery among women, and demand emancipation on the soil, not colonization in the clouds."

Well and happily said, every word of it—Woman should have justice as well as praise; and if she is to dispense with either, she can better afford to part with the latter than the former. It may be that there is something in our position, in this country—something in the injustice of which we are the subjects—something in the hatred of slavery and proscription, either natural or acquired by the hard circumstances of our early life—at any rate, from some cause—this whole woman question is exceedingly plain and simple, and commends itself at once to our mind. Woman, however, like the colored man, will never be taken by her brother and lifted to a position. What she desires, she must fight for. With her as with us, "Who would be free themselves must strike the blow." The price demanded for the good sought, is labor, self-sacrifice, the loss of popularity, loss of the good opinions of men. It is only when the object shall, in estimation, transcend all these that the effort will be commensurated with the conditions of success.

Does woman think she can build a house, and that that is the best appropriation of her time and the best application of her strength and talents? We say, let her go at it, and let shame fall upon the man who would hinder by word or dead, the laudable undertaking. But we repeat woman must practically as well as theoretically, assert her rights. She must *do*, as well as *be*. A Doctor Harriet K. Hunt, a Reverend Antoinette L. Brown or a Mrs. Paulina Davis, all actively exercising the rights for which they contend, are proof against a world's sophistry and a world's ridicule. It is only in the heat of battle that balls lose their terror. So far as employments are concerned, the coast is comparatively clear, and woman can manage the matter for herself. But not so in the matter of voting. Men must do the work here.—They must, like true men and true Democrats, batter down the thick walls erected against woman at the ballot box, and let taxation and representation go together.

Frederick Douglass' Paper, 10 June 1853

The Just and Equal Rights of Women

To the Men and Women of New York:

The "Woman's Rights" Movement is a practical one, demanding prompt and efficient action for the relief of oppressive wrongs; and, as the Conventions held for several years past, in different States, have answered their end of arousing earnest public attention, the time has come for calling upon the People to reform the evils from which women suffer, by their Representatives in Legislative Assemblies.

The wise and humane of all classes in society, however much they may differ upon speculative points as to Woman's Nature and Function, agree that there are actual abuses of women, tolerated by custom and authorized by law, which are condemned alike by the genius of Republican Institutions and the spirit of the Christian Religion. Conscience and common sense, then, unite to sanction their immediate redress. Thousands of the best men and women, in all our communities, are asking such questions as these:

1. Why should not Woman's work be paid for according to the "quality" of the work done, and not the sex of the worker?

2. How shall we open for Woman's energies new spheres of well-remunerated industry?

3. Why should not Wives, equally with Husbands, be entitled to their own earnings?

4. Why should not Widows, equally with Widowers, become by

law the legal guardians, as they certainly are by nature the natural Guardians, of their own children?

5. On what just ground do the laws make a distinction between Man and Woman, in regard to the ownership of property, inheritance, and the administration of estates?

6. Why should Women, any more than Men, be taxed without representation?

7. Why may not Women claim to be tried by a jury of their peers, with exactly the same right as Men claim to be and actually are?

8. If Women need the protection of the laws, and are subject to the penalties of the laws equally with Men, why should they not have an equal influence in making the Laws, and appointing Legislatures, the Judiciary, and Executive?

And finally, if Governments,—according to our National Declaration of Independence,—"derive their just powers from the consent of the governed," why should Women, any more than Men be governed without their own consent; and why, therefore, is not Woman's right to Suffrage precisely equal to Man's!

For the end of finding out practical answers to these and similar questions, and making suitable arrangements to bring the existing "wrongs of Woman," in the State of New York, before the Legislature at its next session,—we, the undersigned, do urgently request the Men and Women of the Commonwealth to assemble in Convention, in this city of Rochester, on Wednesday, November 9th, and Thursday, December 1st, 1853.

(Signed) Frederick Douglass, Elizabeth Cady Stanton, Susan B. Anthony, etc.

Frederick Douglass' Paper, 25 November 1853

Woman's Rights: Circulate the Petitions

The design of the Convention held last week in Rochester, was to bring the subject of Woman's legal and civil disabilities, in a dignified form, before the Legislature of New York.

Convinced, as the friends of the movement are, that inconsistency with the principle of republicanism, females equally with males, are entitled to Freedom, Representation and Suffrage; and, confident as they are that Woman's influence will be found to be as refining and elevating in public, as all experience proves it to be in private, they claim that *one half* of the people and citizens of New York should no longer be governed by the other half, without consent asked and given.

Encouraged by reforms already made in the barbarous usages of Common Law, by the statutes of New York, the advocates of Woman's just and equal rights demand that this work of reform be completed, until every vestige of *partiality* be removed. It is proposed, in a carefully prepared Address to specify the remaining legal disabilities, from which the women of this State yet suffer; and a hearing is asked before a Joint Committee of both Houses, specially empowered to revise and amend the statutes.

Now is this movement right in principle? Is it wise in policy?

Should the females of New York be placed on a level of equality with males before the law? If so, let us petition for this impartial justice to women.

In order to insure this equal justice should the females of New York, like the males, have a voice in appointing the law makers and the law administrators? If so, let us petition for Woman's Right to Suffrage.

Finally, what candid man will be opposed to a reference of the whole subject to the Representatives of New York, whom the Men of New York themselves elected. Let us then petition for a *hearing* before the Legislature.

One word more, as to the Petitions, given below. They are *two* in number; one for the JUST AND EQUAL RIGHTS OF WOMEN; one for WOMAN'S RIGHT TO SUFFRAGE. It is designed that they should be signed by men and women of *lawful age*—that is of twenty-one years and upward. The following directions are suggested:

1. Let persons, ready and willing, sign *each* of the petitions; but let not those who desire to secure Woman's Just and Equal Rights, hesitate to sign that petition, because they have doubts as to the right and expediency of Woman's voting. The petitions will be kept separate, and offered separately. All fair-minded persons, of both sexes, ought to sign the *first* petition. We trust that many thousands are prepared to sign the *second* also.

2. In obtaining signatures, let men sign in one column, and women in another parallel column.

3. Let the name of the town and county, together with the number of signatures, be distinctly entered on the Petitions before they are returned.

4. Let every person, man or woman, interested in this movement, instantly and energetically circulate the petitions in their respective neighborhoods. We must send in the name of every person in the State, who desires full justice to woman, so far as it is possible. Up then friends, and be doing, *today*.

5. Let no person sign either petition, but *once*. As many persons will circulate petitions in the same town and county, it is important to guard against this *possible abuse*.

6. Finally, let every petition be returned to Rochester, directed to the Secretary of the Convention, Susan B. Anthony, on the first of February, without fail.

Petition for the Just and Equal Rights of Women

The Legislature of the State of New York have, by the Acts of 1848 and 1849, testified the purpose of the People of this State to place Married Women on an equality with Married Men in regard to the holding, and devising of real and personal property.

We, therefore, the undersigned petitioners, inhabitants of the State of New York, male and female, having attained the age of legal majority, believing that Women, alike married and single, do still suffer under many and grievous legal disabilities, do earnestly request the Senate and Assembly of the State of New York to appoint a Joint Committee of both houses, to revise the Statutes of New York, and to propose such amendments as will fully establish the legal equality of Women and Men; and do hereby ask a hearing before such Committee by our accredited Representatives.

Petition for Women's Right to Suffrage

Whereas, according to the Declaration of our National Independence, Governments derive their just powers from the consent of the governed, we earnestly request the Legislature of New York to

propose to the people of the State such amendments of the Constitution of the State as will secure to Females an equal right to the
Elective Franchise with Males; and we hereby request a hearing
before the Legislature by our accredited representatives.

Frederick Douglass' Paper, 25 December 1853

EXPLANATORY NOTES

3 *Preface*: this preface is by William Lloyd Garrison (1805–79), radical abolitionist, journalist, and social reformer. He was principal founder of the Massachusetts and American Anti-Slavery societies and the editor of *The Liberator* (1831–65), an anti-slavery journal.

New Bedford: Douglass settled in New Bedford, Massachusetts after escaping from Baltimore on 3 September 1838.

universal liberty!: Garrisonian reformers saw abolitionism as inseparably bound to a programme of 'universal emancipation', including women's rights, Native American rights, pacifism, and temperance.

"gave the world ... a MAN": William Shakespeare, *Hamlet*, III. iv. 62. Hamlet describes his father to Gertrude as 'A combination and a form, indeed, | Where every god did seem to set his seal, | To give the world assurance of a man.'

4 *"created ... lower than the angels"*: Ps. 8: 5: God 'hast made [man] a little lower than the angels'. Paul explains to the Hebrews that Christ was made 'little lower than the angels'.

A beloved friend: William C. Coffin, a prominent New Bedford abolitionist.

PATRICK HENRY: (1736–99), American orator and political leader, best known for his words, 'I do not know what course others may take, but as for me, give me liberty or give me death.'

5 *old Bay State?*: a nickname for Massachusetts, from its former name, The Colony of Massachusetts Bay.

northern prejudice: northern racism was so strong that it prompted Douglass to state in an early speech that 'Prejudice against color is stronger north than south; it hangs around my neck like a heavy weight'.

JOHN A. COLLINS: (1810–79), a controversial abolitionist and social reformer, he resigned as general agent of the Massachusetts Anti-Slavery Society to found a commune based on the anti-property philosophy of Fourierism.

"grow in grace ... of God": St Peter (2 Pet. 3: 18) warns that this world will be destroyed and prays that the faithful will 'grow in grace and in the knowledge of God'.

6 *CHARLES LENOX REMOND*: (1810–73), a free-born black abolitionist and social reformer, he was the first lecturer for the Massachusetts Anti-Slavery Society and was well known in both America and Europe.

DANIEL O'CONNELL: (1775–1847), Irish political leader and advocate of

Catholic emancipation and Irish independence. Known as 'the Liberator'.

Loyal National Repeal Association: organization formed by Daniel O'Connell to promote the restoration of the Irish parliament and the repeal of the union of Great Britain and Ireland.

7 *"in slaves and the souls of men"*: St John predicts the fall of Babylon, where 'the merchants of the earth' buy and sell 'slaves and souls of men' (Rev. 18: 11, 13).

8 *Alexandrian library*: the most famous library of antiquity, begun in the third century BC in Egypt and destroyed in the late third century AD. It was the centre of Greek literary and historical scholarship.

10 *slave code*: these, sometimes referred to as 'black codes', were the separate laws for slaves and freedmen designed to protect whites and perpetuate slavery.

11 *"NO COMPROMISE . . . WITH SLAVEHOLDERS!"*: Garrison advocated disunion, arguing that the Free states should break with slaveholding states.

12 *WENDELL PHILLIPS, ESQ.*: (1811–84), renowned abolitionist and universal reformer. President of the American Anti-Slavery Society (1865–70).

West India experiment: slavery was abolished throughout the British Empire in 1833; by 1838 the emancipation process was complete.

13 *"noon of night"*: compare Matt. 27: 45: 'From midday a darkness fell over the whole land . . . [and Jesus cried aloud] "My God, my God, why hast thou forsaken me?"'.

14 *"hide the outcast"*: see Isa. 16: 3: 'Hide the outcast, do not betray the fugitive.'

15 *during 1835, I was about seventeen years old*: historians have found records dating Douglass's birth as February 1818.

17 *God cursed Ham*: in Gen. 9: 20–27, Ham sees Noah, his father, naked. Noah curses Ham, condemning him and his descendants to be slaves to his brothers, Shem and Japheth. Apologists for slavery cited this passage as biblical authority for slavery.

18 *cowskin*: a whip made of rough leather.

24 *"there is no . . . heart"*: from *The Task* (1785), by British author, William Cowper (1731–1800). This line is from a section of the poem that attacks slavery, declaring 'I had much rather be myself the slave | And wear the bonds, than fasten them on him.'

26 *touching tar without being defiled*: compare the early American proverb, 'He that touches pitch shall be defiled.'

dearborns and barouches: different types of carriages.

27 *riches of Job*: Job's wealth was 'greater than any of the men of the East' (Job 1: 3).

40 *gip!*: American slang for a female dog; bitch.

44 *"The Columbian orator"*: its full title was 'The Columbian Orator: A Variety of Original and Selected Pieces; Together with Rules; Calculated to Improve Youth and Others in the Ornamental and Useful Art of Eloquence' (1797), a collection of patriotic speeches, classic poems, playlets, and dialogues compiled by Caleb Bingham. Bingham reprinted the 'dialogue between a master and his slave' from a collection of writings for youth titled 'Evenings at Home, or The juvenile budget opened: consisting of a variety of miscellaneous pieces for the instruction and amusement of young Persons', by John Aikin and Anna Barbauld, published in six volumes, between 1792 and 1796.

Sheridan's mighty speeches: Douglass refers to the speech by Arthur O'Connor (1763–1852). Richard Sheridan (1751–1816) was a famous Irish playwright and political leader.

"Catholic emancipation": in 1829 the British government reluctantly granted Roman Catholics improved civil rights, including access to most political offices.

46 *scow*: a flat-bottomed boat designed to carry bulk materials.

47 *Webster's Spelling Book*: refers to the *American Spelling Book* (1783) by Noah Webster (1758–1843), leading American lexicographer of his day.

50 *Whittier*: John Greenleaf Whittier (1807–92), American Quaker, poet, and abolitionist. The quoted lines are from 'The Farewell of a Virginia Slave Mother to Her Daughters, Sold into Southern Bondage' (1838).

51 *Will not . . . for these things?*: compare Jer. 5: 9, 29: 'Shall I not visit for these things? saith the Lord. Shall not my soul be avenged on such a nation as this?' This verse appears in full in the appendix to the *Narrative*.

54 *smoke-house*: storage house for preserving meat and fish.

55 *camp-meeting*: an outdoor evangelical revival gathering where worshippers encamped in rural areas.

56 *"He that knoweth . . . beaten with many stripes"*: Luke 12: 47.

59 *saving-fodder time*: harvest time.

binding blades: gathering crops into bundles.

60 *like a thief in the night*: compare 1 Thess. 5: 2, 'the day of the Lord is coming like a thief in the night.'

63 *clearing . . . before the fan*: the separation of wheat from dirt and chaff.

77 *"rather bear . . . knew not of"*: William Shakespeare, *Hamlet*, III. i. 81–2.

84 *"Hurra, Fred.!"*: i.e. hurry.

bowse: to lift or haul with a rope and tackle.

94 *DAVID RUGGLES*: (1810–49), Ruggles was a free-born abolitionist and journalist who helped Douglass escape from Maryland.

Darg case: Ruggles was arrested in 1839, but never prosecuted, for harbouring Thomas Hughes, a fugitive slave, who had escaped from John P. Darg of Arkansas.

95 *Anna, my intended wife*: Anna Murray (1813?–82), who was free, helped finance Douglass's trip from her wages as a domestic worker. Little is known of their courtship.

Rev. J. W. C. Pennington: Pennington (1807–70) escaped from slavery in 1831 to become a pastor, abolitionist orator, teacher, and author.

96 *"Lady of the Lake" ... "Douglass"*: a central character in Sir Walter Scott's (1771–1832) *Lady of the Lake* (1810), Douglass is the wrongfully banished Lord James of Douglas.

98 *"I was hungry ... he took me in"*: Matt. 25: 35.

99 *hod*: wooden trough with a handle, borne on the shoulder, for carrying heavy items such as brick and mortar.

101 *"stealing the livery ... to serve the devil in"*: compare Scottish poet Robert Pollok's (1798–1827) *The Course of Time* (1827), book 8, lines 616–18: 'He was a man | Who stole the livery of the court of Heaven | To serve the Devil in.'

102 *ark of light*: the Ark of the Covenant held the Torah, Moses' book of the law, and represented great holiness. To lay impure hands on the Ark was a serious crime: God slew Uzzah for doing so (2 Sam. 6: 6–7).

103 *Pilate and Herod friends!*: Pontius Pilate was the Roman governor of Judea, who sentenced Jesus to crucifixion. Herod Antipas was ruler of Galilee and Perea, and is best known for executing John the Baptist. Pilate and Herod (former enemies) became friends through their agreement to condemn Christ to death (Luke 23: 12).

"Just God ... spoiler thine?": the above stanzas are taken from Whittier's anti-slavery poem, 'Clerical Oppressors' (1836).

scribes and Pharisees: Christ condemned the scribes and Pharisees for observing the letter, while ignoring the spirit of the law. The scribes copied, interpreted, and taught the Jewish scriptures; the Pharisees were a formalist religious sect that stressed the strict observance of legal rites and ceremonies.

104 *"Shall I not ... nation as this?"*: Jer. 5: 9.

A PARODY: mimicking a popular Southern hymn, 'Heavenly Union'.

105 *Bashan bull*: Bashan was a region east of the river Jordan; its bulls were famed for their strength.

The Oxford World's Classics Website

www.worldsclassics.co.uk

- Browse the full range of Oxford World's Classics online

- Sign up for our monthly e-alert to receive information on new titles

- Read extracts from the Introductions

- Listen to our editors and translators talk about the world's greatest literature with our Oxford World's Classics audio guides

- Join the conversation, follow us on Twitter at OWC_Oxford

- Teachers and lecturers can order inspection copies quickly and simply via our website

www.worldsclassics.co.uk

American Literature

British and Irish Literature

Children's Literature

Classics and Ancient Literature

Colonial Literature

Eastern Literature

European Literature

Gothic Literature

History

Medieval Literature

Oxford English Drama

Poetry

Philosophy

Politics

Religion

The Oxford Shakespeare

A complete list of Oxford World's Classics, including Authors in Context, Oxford English Drama, and the Oxford Shakespeare, is available in the UK from the Marketing Services Department, Oxford University Press, Great Clarendon Street, Oxford OX2 6DP, or visit the website at www.oup.com/uk/worldsclassics.

In the USA, visit www.oup.com/us/owc for a complete title list.

Oxford World's Classics are available from all good bookshops. In case of difficulty, customers in the UK should contact Oxford University Press Bookshop, 116 High Street, Oxford OX1 4BR.

GEORGE ELIOT	Adam Bede
	Daniel Deronda
	Middlemarch
	The Mill on the Floss
	Silas Marner
ELIZABETH GASKELL	Cranford
	The Life of Charlotte Brontë
	Mary Barton
	North and South
	Wives and Daughters
THOMAS HARDY	Far from the Madding Crowd
	Jude the Obscure
	The Mayor of Casterbridge
	A Pair of Blue Eyes
	The Return of the Native
	Tess of the d'Urbervilles
	The Woodlanders
WALTER SCOTT	Ivanhoe
	Rob Roy
	Waverley
MARY SHELLEY	Frankenstein
	The Last Man
ROBERT LOUIS STEVENSON	Kidnapped and Catriona
	The Strange Case of Dr Jekyll and Mr Hyde and Weir of Hermiston
	Treasure Island
BRAM STOKER	Dracula
WILLIAM MAKEPEACE THACKERAY	Barry Lyndon
	Vanity Fair
OSCAR WILDE	Complete Shorter Fiction
	The Picture of Dorian Gray

ANTHONY TROLLOPE

An Autobiography

Ayala's Angel

Barchester Towers

The Belton Estate

The Bertrams

Can You Forgive Her?

The Claverings

Cousin Henry

Doctor Thorne

Doctor Wortle's School

The Duke's Children

Early Short Stories

The Eustace Diamonds

An Eye for an Eye

Framley Parsonage

He Knew He Was Right

Lady Anna

The Last Chronicle of Barset

Later Short Stories

Miss Mackenzie

Mr Scarborough's Family

Orley Farm

Phineas Finn

Phineas Redux

The Prime Minister

Rachel Ray

The Small House at Allington

La Vendée

The Warden

The Way We Live Now